Stude

A...

BY D...

THE AUTHOR

Dr Dominique Thompson is a GP, young people's mental health expert, TEDx speaker, author and educator, with over 20 years of clinical experience caring for students, most recently as Director of Service at the University of Bristol Students' Health Service. It was for this work that she was named Bristol Healthcare Professional of the Year 2017.

She is a Clinical Advisor for the Royal College of GPs, and for Student Minds, the UK's student mental health charity. She was the GP member of the NICE Eating Disorders' guidelines development group, and the Universities UK StepChange and Minding Our Future committees. Dominique is also a member of the UK Mental Wellbeing in Higher Education group (MWBHE).

Dominique's TEDx talk, What I learnt from 78,000 GP consultations with university students, highlights some of the causes behind the recent rise in young people's mental health distress, and suggests ways in which everyone can better support the younger generation.

You can follow her on twitter @DrdomThompson and on Instagram as drdom99

Contributing Editor Lauren Callaghan (CPsychol, PGDipClinPsych, PgCert, MA (hons), LLB (hons), BA) is a clinical psychologist who specialises in CBT and has over 15 years' experience of working with adults and young people, including students. She has worked at national-level specialist CBT services in the UK and has taught and tutored trainee therapists in CBT, as well as providing guest lectures and tutoring for University CBT training courses. She is a frequent guest speaker on mental health conditions in the media and at academic conferences and is the is the author of a number of self-help books on anxiety and obsessional problems, including books which are available on prescription in the UK. Lauren is now based in London, where she set up and now runs a specialist CBT clinic. She is passionate about mental health and improving access to good quality treatments, and to this end she co-founded Trigger Publishing, a publishing company focused solely on mental health publications. In addition, Lauren is a co-founder, trustee and clinical director of the Shaw Mind Foundation charity.

First published in Great Britain 2019 by Trigger

The Foundation Centre
Navigation House, 48 Millgate, Newark
Nottinghamshire NG24 4TS UK

www.triggerpublishing.com

British Library Cataloguing in Publication Data

A CIP catalogue record for this book is available upon
request from the British Library

ISBN: 978-1-78956-056-5

This book is also available in the following e-Book formats:

MOBI: 978-1-78956-059-6
EPUB: 978-1-78956-057-2
PDF: 978-1-78956-058-9

Cover design and typeset by Fusion Graphic Design Ltd

Printed and bound in Great Britain by Clays Ltd, Elcograf S.p.A

Paper from responsible sources

TRIGGER™

The mental health & wellbeing publisher

www.triggerpublishing.com

Thank you for purchasing this book.
You are making an incredible difference.

Proceeds from all Trigger books go directly to
The Shaw Mind Foundation, a global charity that focuses
entirely on mental health. To find out more about
The Shaw Mind Foundation, visit
www.shawmindfoundation.org

MISSION STATEMENT

Our goal is to make help and support available for every
single person in society, from all walks of life. We will
never stop offering hope. These are our promises.

Trigger and The Shaw Mind Foundation

the *Shaw* mind
FOUNDATION

Creating hope for children,
adults and families

*For Steph, thank you for everything,
and remember, you can do this!*

ROLE DEFINITIONS

A Who's Who of Student Support

GP (general practitioner)

A GP is a medically qualified doctor who sees people in the community, not in a hospital. They are able to help with all conditions, although they may have a special interest, for example in skin problems or mental health. They are sometimes called "family doctors," and will often refer to specialists, such as psychiatrists or psychologists, for specific problems.

Counsellor

A counsellor offers a safe confidential space for individuals to talk. Counsellors help their clients explore their thoughts, feelings and actions to help them come to terms with life and find more hopeful and useful ways to approach their future. Counsellors will work in different ways depending on their training, but will always allow their client to take the lead in what they want to talk about. They do not offer advice, but through the empathic attention they give to their client's words, the client often discovers their own wisdom, helping them to lead a more fulfilling life.

Clinical Psychologist

A person who specialises in psychological or emotional conditions and mental health disorders. They will have specialised in the study of clinical psychology and will usually have a doctorate or PHD (though they're not medically qualified and will not able to prescribe medication). They assess people and diagnose mental health conditions or problems. They are trained in using talking and behavioural interventions specifically tailored to treat psychological disorders. They may use a range of therapy approaches which vary from psychodynamic to cognitive behavioural therapy and family and couples' therapies, to interpersonal approaches. They base their assessment and treatment methods on scientific principles and outcomes, and will use the best evidenced method that helps to treat an individual.

Therapist

A term for professionals who use talking and behavioural therapies to support people with mental health conditions.

Psychiatrist

A medically qualified doctor who specialises in mental health conditions (also called psychiatric conditions) who can assess, make a diagnosis, offer advice, and prescribe medications. A psychiatrist is the only person who can prescribe some specialist medications. They work with GPs, therapists, psychologists and counsellors, and will usually recommend a type of talking or behavioural treatment.

CONTENTS

INTRODUCTION

Anxiety can be exhausting, and it can take over your life. Getting help can feel overwhelming ...

You've taken the first step by picking up this book! Well done.

Keep going ...

Who should read this book

- If you are a worrier
- If you are stressed a lot
- If you get worked up about things
- If you feel like your emotions are a bubbling pot that you are only just keeping a lid on
- If you feel anxious about specific things, or all of the time, to the extent that it stops you from enjoying life or getting things done
- If you have panic attacks
- If you get very anxious in social or group situations
- If you struggle with repetitive intrusive thoughts, ruminations, or compulsive behaviours that you can't control
- If you know someone who fits these descriptions, and you want to better understand what they are going through

- If you work with people who suffer from anxiety problems or phobias and want to be able to support them better

Why you should read this book

- To learn more about what anxiety is
- To understand why it causes certain feelings
- To learn about some of the causes
- To work out if you have an anxiety problem
- To know when and where to get help, and who to speak to about it
- To better understand what help might be available, and what might help you
- To tackle some of the myths around anxiety
- To know what to try for yourself that could help, and to avoid what could make it worse
- To understand which treatments or therapies are recommended for different types of anxiety problems
- To get a sense of which medications are available, and what you might be offered if appropriate
- To know where to get further help
- To know you are not alone

CHAPTER 1

WHAT IS ANXIETY?

A lot of people have anxiety. It's actually the commonest problem that students talk to university counselling services about, and it's the second most common mental health topic that students talk to their doctor about, after depression (Thorley, 2017). In fact, these days, a lot of people are talking about their experience of anxiety online, or writing books about it, which means that there is a lot of information out there; some of it very reassuring, but also some of it may not be right for you. Hopefully this book will help you to sort out what you need to know, and what could help you, when there is so much info available (which in itself could make you feel anxious).

 Anxiety is the second most common mental health condition in the world, with 275 million people affected (Our world in data, 2018)

How do I know if I have anxiety?
Anxiety can mean different things to different people and can be experienced in a number of ways.
- It can feel like a "rock" in the pit of your stomach
- It can feel like "butterflies" or a "sick" feeling
- It can make you shaky

- It could make you feel as if you have a permanent sense of dread, that something bad is about to happen *all the time*
- It can make it difficult for you to get to sleep, or sleep through the night
- It can affect your concentration
- You may get sweaty or tremble
- You may cry more easily or feel more irritable
- The feelings can be physical, emotional or both
- You may want to hide and stay in bed, or create a duvet "nest" to feel safe in
- Leaving familiar places can feel terrifying
- Doing ordinary things, like getting a bus, can feel too much or be overwhelming
- You may feel anxious all the time, or you may just feel anxiety when something specific is worrying you, such as an exam or a presentation to a group of people.

People experience anxiety in different ways.

Physical symptoms of anxiety
- Increased heart rate or "palpitations"
- Fast, shallow breathing
- Shaking / trembling
- Feeling hot
- Sweating
- Chest pains
- Diarrhoea
- Feeling sick / vomiting
- Abdominal pain / cramps
- Headaches
- Dizzy spells

- Muscle tension / tightness / aches
- Dry mouth
- Jitteriness / restlessness
- Tingly hands, feet or face
- Prickly skin or scalp
- Teeth grinding

 People with anxiety tend to sway more, which may explain their dizzy spells
(Examined Existence, 2018)

Emotional symptoms of anxiety
- Feel fearful, worried, or apprehensive
- Feeling "on edge"
- Feeling disconnected from yourself or the physical world around you
- Mood swings
- A sense of dread
- Irritability / anger
- Feeling scared

Behavioural symptoms of anxiety
- Unable to relax
- Poor sleep
- Poor concentration / focus
- Ruminating, which is going over things in your mind again and again
- Seeking constant reassurance from others
- Scanning people, environments, or yourself even for things that might make you fearful
- Avoidance of difficult situations

- Using alcohol or drugs to try to reduce or cover up the anxiety
- Developing safety behaviours – these are usually counter-productive behaviours designed to stop the thing you are worried about from happening

Cognitive symptoms

- Thinking that the worst thing that can happen, *will* happen (known as catastrophising)
- Overestimating the risk of bad things happening
- Going over and over past events in your head (ruminating)
- Overthinking future events and possible outcomes
- Unpleasant images, thoughts or doubts popping into your head
- Trying to predict what might happen (forecasting the future)
- Planning an "escape" from a feared situation
- Scanning your body for symptoms of anxiety
- Scanning the environment for "risky" events, places or things
- Being self-critical or self-blaming

 'Everyone experiences a version of anxiety or worry in their lives, and maybe we go through it in a different or more intense way for longer periods of time, but there's nothing wrong with you.' **Emma Stone, actress** (*My Body and Soul*, 2017)

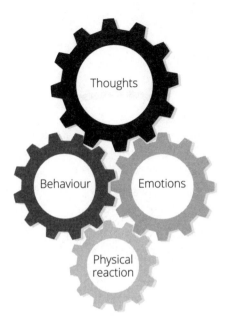

Figure 1: *The interaction of our thoughts, emotions, behaviours and physiological reactions.*

The vicious cycle of anxiety

If you want to get an idea of what's going on for you in stressful situations, take a look at this diagram. It shows how your thoughts, feelings, responses and behaviours interact to create a vicious cycle of unhelpful thoughts.

Anxiety often feeds upon itself. Because we worry about things, we either avoid doing things or we do some safety behaviours to prevent the bad thing happening, or to avoid our exposure to it – but ironically, this only increases our anxiety over time.

This is Adam

Adam is a first year student and worries a lot about what people think about him.

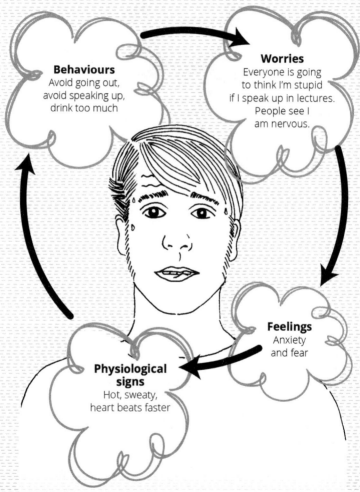

Behaviours
Avoid going out, avoid speaking up, drink too much

Worries
Everyone is going to think I'm stupid if I speak up in lectures. People see I am nervous.

Feelings
Anxiety and fear

Physiological signs
Hot, sweaty, heart beats faster

Adam experiences some physiological signs – he notices feeling hot and sweaty, and his heart beats faster.

So how do these feelings affect him? He avoids putting his hand up to speak in lectures. And he avoids going to parties when he can. If he does go to parties, he drinks too much to numb his worries.

What he hasn't done is disprove the worry that people will think he's stupid, or notice his anxiety. He has just avoided it, which only makes it seem more likely that his fears will come true. As you can see, by avoiding doing these things or covering up his worry with alcohol, he doesn't find out what happens if he does speak out in lectures or go to parties sober. In turn, this gives more power to his worries, so he thinks they are still likely to happen. This is an example of a vicious cycle of anxiety.

> **Try this for yourself**
> Have a think about what causes your anxiety and how it makes you feel when you have these worries both emotionally and physiologically, and what you do or don't do because of these worries.

Anxiety and physical conditions

It is very important to remember that anxiety not only causes lots of physical feelings and sensations (symptoms) but it is closely linked to many physical conditions (El-Gabalawy et al., 2011 and Scott et al., 2007) and may cause them to get worse, for example, irritable bowel syndrome, migraine, fibromyalgia, chronic back pain and asthma. As having these conditions can also make us feel more anxious, it can be a bit of a vicious cycle, unfortunately. So addressing our anxiety becomes even more important as a way to look after our overall health.

Worries
What makes
me anxious?

Behaviours
What do I do; what do I not
do because of these worries?

Feelings
How do I
feel emotionally?

**Physiological
signs**
How I feel and what
I notice in my body

This book will cover all of these things, and together we will try to find ways to help you manage your own anxiety, whatever shape it takes.

This book will tell you what you need to know if you have anxiety.

'One cannot fight what one does not know.'
Rollo May (*The Meaning of Anxiety*,1977) p. 207

This book will help you find ways to deal with your anxiety, so that it doesn't ruin your time at uni. Stick with it and it should help you to feel a lot calmer, have a better understanding of what's happening, and be more in control of your feelings, with some helpful, practical tips and advice.

Every year 40 million adults in the USA are affected by anxiety (Adaa.org, 2018)

CHAPTER 2

TELL ME MORE ABOUT ANXIETY

Why do we humans get anxious? And is it all bad?

It can be helpful to remind ourselves where anxiety and feeling worried (or "stressed") about things comes from, in evolutionary terms. People use the words "anxiety", "worry" and "stress" interchangeably, and to mean the same thing, though from a medical or technical point of view "anxiety" is used most often.

Fight or flight

As humans, our number one priority, in the most basic terms, is to stay alive. To do this, over hundreds of thousands of years, we have developed incredible internal systems to survive in the face of danger. We call the response produced by these internal systems the "fight or flight" response. Brilliant (and potentially life-saving) when faced with a sabre-toothed tiger, or jumping out of the way of a speeding pavement cyclist; less brilliant when trying to study in the library or plan a day out with friends.

The "fight or flight" response goes something like this (Harvard Publishing, 2018):

Our eyes and ears pick up on "danger" and send signals to the brain.

The command centre in the brain sends out distress signals to our nervous system.

These signals reach the adrenal glands (on top of our kidneys) which pump out adrenaline, and this life-saving hormone is carried around the body to a whole variety of other organs, via the blood stream.

Your organs then respond to the danger in ways designed to save your life and make you super-alert ...

What does your body do next?

Your lungs – you breathe faster to take in more oxygen, to help you think quickly, and assist your muscles (you become "breathless" with fear)

Your heart – beats faster to pump around blood (containing oxygen and adrenaline) to your muscles and brain ("heart racing")

Your brain – becomes hyper alert and aware of your surroundings ("alert to danger")

Your eyes – the pupils dilate to let in more light and allow for a bigger field of vision, to scan for danger ("wide-eyed" with fright), but this can also make you "dizzy with fear"

Your bowels – want to empty (diarrhoea) to make you lighter when you run ("he soiled himself in terror")

Your stomach – wants to empty (vomit), again to lighten the load ("sick with fear")

Your muscles – fill with blood to help you move away from danger fast

You sweat – to reduce the risk of overheating with all this extra activity going on, and from the anticipated running away ("hands slick with fear")

You shake – this may be a side effect of not "using up" the flood of energy produced by the adrenaline, in other words, if you were to run away you probably wouldn't shake, or it may be the muscles preparing to run ("tremble" with fear)

Your hair – "standing on end" to make you appear big and scary, and making your scalp "prickle"

Suddenly you can see how all of these reactions might be really useful in times of genuine danger to life, when you need to think and move fast, but less so when trying to catch the bus or go to the shops. Yet for many people, anxiety, and in some cases panic attacks (short episodes of extreme anxiety), have become a part of their lives and create a significant amount of distress and may also prevent people from engaging in normal activities.

'Anxiety is a kind of fuel that activates the fight-or-flight part of the brain in me. It makes sure that a velociraptor isn't around the corner and that you do as much as you possibly can to survive.'
Ben Affleck, actor (*Hollywood Reporter*, 2012)

So, it may be helpful to think of anxiety, and panic attacks, as an over the top "fight or flight" response, an overreaction to perceived danger or threat.

The body creates a stress reaction when it doesn't need to, but it is not easily in your control to stop it from happening.

However, there are steps you can take to regain confidence and cope better, and one of the aims of this book is to support you to do that.

It won't necessarily be easy, but it is absolutely possible to overcome anxiety to the point that you can live an active life, doing the things you want to do. It may take a bit of time, and quite a lot of effort in some cases, but it will be worth it. You can do this!

'I have anxiety attacks, constant panicking on stage, my heart feels like it's going to explode because I never feel like I'm going to deliver, ever.' **Adele, singer** (*Stylist*, 2016)

And remember … it is important that you do experience stress or an adrenaline rush in certain circumstances. Not just because it can save your life, but because it can help you focus in challenging situations, so that you are hyped up and firing on all cylinders when you need to be. For example, for an important exam or for a job interview. You need this response to be manageable, but you wouldn't want to be without it completely.

In other words, some anxiety is good for us, but we need to be in control of it, not have it be in control of us!

In 2013 there were 8.2 million cases of anxiety in the UK (mind.org.uk, 2018)

CHAPTER 3

TYPES OF ANXIETY

It may be helpful to think of the word "anxiety" as the broad umbrella term under which many "types" of anxiety and some obsessional disorders are clustered. For example,

- Phobias (disproportionate or unreasonable fears of particular things or activities, like snakes, clowns, or flying)
- Obsessional problems such as *obsessive compulsive disorders*, which are characterised by obsessive worries, and related behaviours
- Health anxiety (obsessive concern and worrying or rumination about their own health)
- Body Dysmorphic Disorder, which causes people to believe that a part of their body is deeply flawed, or abnormal.

Most people have a more *general* anxiety, not related to specific triggers or causes.

Coming up is a list of the different types of anxiety problems, and it may be helpful for you to know what you have. The good news is that the approaches to managing and treating them are all pretty similar, so, as long as you seek professional help,

About **half** of those who have anxiety also have depression

PHOBIAS
Panic Disorder
ACUTE STRESS REACTION
Social Anxiety Disorder
Generalised Anxiety Disorder
OBSESSIVE COMPULSIVE DISORDER

e.g. via a doctor (GP), counsellor or psychologist, you will be pointed in the right direction, whatever "type" you are struggling with. The key is to *seek help*, and not ignore it or hope it will go away by itself (it most likely won't if it has lasted a while, or keeps coming back).

It may also be helpful to know that many people will develop anxiety at some point in their life, perhaps in response to a difficult situation, like a relationship breakdown, or job hunting, but that they will recover from this episode and move on, without necessarily developing a long-term anxiety problem or disorder. They may still need support, counselling, or some treatment to get them through it, but they are likely to get back to normal. In future months or years they may have another episode, but they are probably going to recognise it sooner for what it is, know when and how to get help if needed, and recover well again, if they don't ignore it.

This book will mainly be referring to the disorders listed below (icd.who.int, 2018), although there are other, less common conditions that may affect people and cause similar symptoms. This book may still be helpful for rarer types of obsessional and anxiety problems, such as Body Dysmorphic Disorder.

Phobias

Phobias occur when someone is frightened of something which most people would not be worried about, such as flying or ladders. The fear is disproportionate to the threat posed by the object of fear. In other words, it might be normal to be scared of a rapidly approaching great white shark when open sea swimming, but not of a tiny mouse running across the floor!

Students often seek help for fear of flying before their year abroad or the summer holidays, and some medical and dental students have been known to seek help for blood or needle phobias. Although some phobias appear to be more common than others, you can develop a phobia about absolutely anything!

Social anxiety disorder

Social anxiety disorder is a persistent fear in which you worry about being scrutinised by others, and it can have similar frightening physical and emotional effects (rcpsych.ac.uk, 2018). You can see how difficult life as a student might be if you have a fear of being with other people, or being judged in a negative way, and yet a remarkable number of students do have social anxiety disorder, though it is often undiagnosed. So it is really important to get help and advice if you recognise this issue in yourself. It doesn't have to be like this! Treatment is available, usually through talking therapies, and for some types of phobias recovery can even be very quick, with just a few sessions required.

People with anxiety may be better at picking up changes in facial expressions, but they may be worse at interpreting the meaning – so they may jump to the wrong conclusions about people's intentions or moods (Chris Fraley et al., 2006)

How do I know if I have social anxiety disorder?

Lots of people feel awkward in group or social situations, but on the whole, they probably don't let it stop them from doing what they want or need to do.

Ask yourself the following two questions (NICE guidance) and if you answer "yes" to either, consider having a conversation with a doctor, or your local psychology service, to consider talking therapies, or possibly medication.

- Do you find yourself avoiding social situations or activities?
- Are you fearful or embarrassed in social situations?

Real life example

Jake was a 19-year-old undergraduate when he first saw the university health centre doctor about his worries. He had been at university for six months but was really struggling to settle in and make friends. He lived in a university hall of residence, but found meeting his fellow residents very challenging, to the extent that he tended to stay in his room, and wait till night time before going into the shared kitchen or bathroom. He would even avoid urinating for hours, in case he might meet someone. He barely attended lectures and tutorials and went online to get his course notes.

He had always been "a shy child" but at home had felt safe. In school, he had one or two friends whom he had known for years and who helped him out, because they knew how difficult he found certain activities, like assemblies, so they would stand one either side of him, to support him emotionally. They had now gone to different universities, and Jake was reaching a real low point, feeling lonely, and thinking of leaving university.

Jake wanted to change; he recognised that it was time to move forwards, but he didn't know how. He wanted to make friends and join in with campus life. He was ready to do something different, but he didn't know what.

Following the meeting with the doctor and an assessment with the local psychology service, Jake was offered a course of Cognitive Behavioural Therapy (CBT) and a review appointment was made with the doctor to see how he was progressing a month later. Medication was discussed in case he might like to try it in future, and he was offered peer support from the university-run peer-to-peer support scheme. This would mean he could get to know a single (trained) fellow student well, as part of his support package.

Jake started his CBT, and, with his peer support student, he slowly made progress, which over the following months allowed him to engage with his residence "corridor buddies", then with his course mates. Six months later he was able to move into a flat with some of his new friends, and to start to feel like he was making the most of his university experience.

Generalised anxiety disorder

This is essentially the name for feeling worried about everything and anything, all of the time (Anxiety UK, 2018). Many students suffer with this, and it can eat into their daily lives, preventing them from functioning as well as they should. For example, they spend so much time worrying about everything that they cannot study, pay attention in lectures, go out with friends or revise. It may not have got to the all-pervasive stage, where you feel worried from the moment you wake up and throughout the day, but if you recognise these features, and a wide variety of things worry you, then it is better to seek help early rather than wait until it gets worse. Treatment is available and successful with talking therapies, as it is for all these conditions, and sometimes tablets can be helpful too, though you won't have to take any if you don't want to. Treatment options will be discussed later on in the book.

Real life example

Cleo was a second-year undergraduate student with a busy modern languages timetable, and lots of social activities. She was involved in the university radio station, and was planning for her year abroad. She was doing well with her studies, getting the grades she needed, and was never without friends around her. But she came to see the university counselling service with a secret. She was extremely anxious. All the time. About everything. She hid it well, from almost everyone, although she had recently told her best friend about it as it was becoming unbearable, and it had been going on for almost a year.

Whether it was planning her radio show each week, writing an essay or discussing what to do with friends on Saturday, she was worrying about it. She was unable to sleep, fretting constantly about all the things that could go wrong, playing out worst-case scenarios, and feeling on edge and tearful, as if something terrible was about to happen. She worried that her friends didn't really like her, that they would think that what she was saying was "stupid" or that people might be laughing at her behind her back. These worries weren't based on any incidents, but she worried about them constantly, obsessing over things she might have said that were silly, or replaying conversations as she felt she "should" have responded. She was exhausted.

The counsellor spent some time with her, exploring her past feelings and emotions, her family history (her mum had been anxious when she was younger), and discussing what Cleo might like to try, to help herself and to take charge of the situation now.

The counsellor talked about generalised anxiety disorder, and gave her some information about it, as well as discussing sleep habits and relaxation techniques. They talked about the possibility of some group work to start to address the symptoms and manage the anxiety. If that was not effective, the counsellor advised that individual talking therapies or CBT might be effective options for addressing anxiety problems.

With the symptoms being so persistent and affecting all aspects of her life, the counsellor advised Cleo to see the university doctor to discuss the possibility of medication, as she was being affected relentlessly by her worries, and the doctor suggested that a low dose antidepressant might be a good option. Cleo left the counselling session feeling relieved and that she had taken a step in the right direction. She would let her family know that she had been struggling, but that she was getting help, so they would feel reassured. Her best friend continued to be supportive and Cleo tried the counselling group. She was surprised to find it really helpful to share her experiences and discover that she was not alone. It helped her to think about new ways to manage her anxiety, from meditation, to changing the demands she put on herself.

The weeks passed and Cleo felt more in control, able to look forward to her year abroad, but aware of the need to keep an eye on her anxiety, and now knowing what to do if it started to become problematic (sleep, eat, exercise, meditate, and get back into a good routine).

Panic disorder

Panic attacks, which are experienced as an overwhelming cascade of symptoms, in particular the physical symptoms of "fight or flight" reactions (see previous section for details), occur with many forms of anxiety disorders, but if they occur on their own, or out of the blue, then we call this "panic disorder" (Anxiety UK, 2018).

The feelings are intense and frightening, and the person having them may genuinely believe that they are going to die or that something terrible is about to happen. It may feel as if the walls are closing in, or you can't breathe, or that you are having a heart attack with chest pain. In fact, a quarter of people who go to A&E with chest pain thinking that they are having a heart attack are in fact having panic symptoms (rcpsych.ac.uk, 2018). So you are not alone. And it can be really frightening. People with panic disorder worry about when they will have another panic attack, and try to avoid anything they think may trigger another one – such as coffee, exercise, going out to certain places, taking public transport, driving, etc. The list is never-ending! Again, treatment is available and effective, so read on to see how you can improve things.

'People use "panic attack" very casually out here in Los Angeles, but I don't think most of them really know what it is. Every breath is laboured. You are dying. You are going to die. It's terrifying. But if you ever experience it, or are experiencing it right now, just know that on the other side, the little joys in life will be that much sweeter. The tough times, the days when you're just a ball on the floor – they'll pass. You're playing the long game and life is totally worth it.'
Sarah Silverman, comedian and actress
(*Glamour*, 2015)

Real life example

Jem was a final year maths undergraduate, with a hectic social life. He was very busy planning his next career steps, with job interviews and internships on the horizon. Anxiety hadn't really been a problem, other than the usual exam nerves, so it came as a huge shock when a few weeks before Finals on the train to an interview Jem felt overwhelmed by feelings of nausea, found himself shaking, feeling dread and fear, and experiencing a real need to get out of his seat and get off the train. Unfortunately the train was speeding along, and there was nowhere to go, which just added to the sense that something terrible was about to happen. Jem got up and staggered to the toilet, where he was

BALI, INDONESIA

PSYCHOLOGY WORK EXPERIENCE HERE

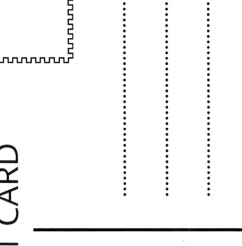

POST CARD

Psychology work experience available.
Passport required.
www.slv.global

sick, and stood shaking till the train reached the next station. He got off, managed to call a friend to collect him, and went home.

Jem had had his first panic attack. But at that stage, he thought that he was suffering with an illness. It was only when the same thing happened again the next time he was on public transport that he started to wonder what was going on, and came to seek professional help. He spoke at length to a university psychological counsellor, trained in mental health issues, and they pieced together the picture: of mounting stress from looming exams, interviews, worries about living arrangements in the future and so on. They talked about how panic attacks are a "fight or flight" reaction, overwhelming us when we don't actually need to be at that level of alertness.

The counsellor shared the fact that public transport is one of the commonest triggers of such panic attacks, and together they planned the best way to manage the panics, and future travelling arrangements.

Jem was made aware of medication options for panic disorder, should he wish to try them. He also understood that while he shouldn't force himself to go into situations that might lead to a panic attack, nor should he completely avoid them, as this would reinforce the fears. In the longer term he planned to start some CBT to tackle the panic disorder, and slowly regain control of his life. He was still able to use public transport, but sometimes had to use some of his new treatment techniques en route. Very occasionally he would not feel up to it, and would have to get off the train or Tube for a bit, then get back on, but he knew he had other treatment options.

Based on what the counsellor told him, Jem planned to start some CBT to tackle the panic disorder and slowly regain control of his life. After just a few sessions of CBT, focusing on panic disorder, Jem made a full recovery and was never bothered by panic attacks again.

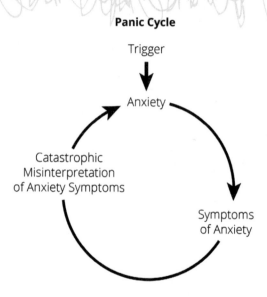

Panic Cycle

Figure 2: Reproduced with kind permission of David Clark.

Obsessive compulsive disorder

Often misinterpreted as a description of super-tidy people, this condition is exhausting and overwhelming, with repetitive thoughts and a relentless feeling that you have to act in certain ways.

This disorder is most easily understood as being in three parts (rcpsych.ac.uk, 2018). First of all, people have *intrusive* thoughts, images, urges, or doubts (obsessions) which cause them anxiety but which they are unable to control. A real life example of an intrusive thought was from a student who worried endlessly that he might inadvertently hurt his girlfriend, causing her severe harm. The anxiety that follows is the second part of the process, which is then followed by the need to carry out certain behaviours (compulsions) or avoid certain things, people or places to try and remove the anxiety created by the thoughts, or prevent the unpleasant thing from happening. The behaviours are carried out to keep the thoughts (and anxiety) in check.

Obsessive thoughts ➜ anxiety ➜ compulsive behaviours

The thoughts are usually that something bad will happen, unless you carry out specific behaviours or avoid certain things in order to prevent the bad thing from happening. For example, that you can prevent a bad thing from happening by not walking on cracks in the pavement, by counting in threes, by touching every fifth letter on a page you are reading or by washing your hands.

The thoughts are very distressing. In some cases, students have been very worried that they might harm someone that they love. They may have intrusive uncontrollable thoughts about this harm, and feel that the only way to control it is by carrying out compulsive behaviours such as checking things (numbers, or words). Sometimes the obsessive thoughts are not followed by external behaviours, so a person may just have very difficult and unpleasant obsessive and repetitive thoughts that they cannot prevent from coming into their mind. They may try other mental strategies to stop the thoughts, e.g. trying to "undo" the bad thought by replacing it with a good one, or pushing it out of their minds. This creates significant distress, but fortunately all these symptoms respond well to talking therapies or CBT and / or medication. Help is available for what is often an extremely distressing condition.

This might be a good time to mention *health anxiety*. Quite a lot of students seek medical advice because of new or unusual symptoms that have been worrying them, such as headaches or diarrhoea. They may have bodily aches and pains, or feel "tingling" sensations. When the doctor takes a thorough history, asking lots of questions and considering what has been happening for the person, it can become apparent that the student has been feeling very stressed or anxious, and has become hyper aware of physical symptoms. However, what happens next is that the student starts to fixate on the physical symptoms, believing them to be caused by a much more serious underlying condition, such as cancer or a neurological problem. For example, they think that their headaches are caused by a brain tumour, or that their tummy aches are an ulcer. Even when all the investigations that the doctor carries out find no serious cause, the student can continue to obsess and worry about the physical symptoms and their possible causes. If one condition is ruled out medically then they tend to move onto another one to worry themselves with. It can become endlessly exhausting and distressing. Health anxiety is part of the Obsessive Compulsive Disorders spectrum and can be treated as such by a course of CBT. Be sure to get some help and advice.

Real life example

Astrid was a post-grad student, living with another student, and working hard on her PhD. Astrid had always been a little anxious, and had a couple of things that she did that helped her to feel in control. For example, she liked her desk arranged in a certain way before she could start work on her laptop, or she would count backwards in threes to calm herself before stressful situations. At home, she had a younger brother, who had always been someone she cared about and looked out for.

As the academic pressure on Astrid increased, she started to become increasingly driven to count things. For example, the words she was writing or the icons on her laptop. She would check things were in the right place or in the right order at home, such as tins in the cupboards or books on the shelf. The more stressed about work she became, the more behaviours started to appear, taking ever more of her time. She was particularly distressed by the feeling that something bad might happen to her brother if she didn't complete the behaviours and rituals. Eventually one night her flatmate found her counting and arranging tins in their kitchen at 2.00am, and encouraged Astrid to seek help from the university support services.

Astrid made an appointment, desperate for help, but unsure what anyone might be able to offer. Following an assessment, and a reassuring and kind conversation with the welfare professional, she felt optimistic about change being possible, with a referral to start CBT and an appointment to discuss the situation with a doctor, in case medication might also be of help.

Astrid was relieved to feel some of the pressure lifting, although aware that it would take time for things to improve. Over the following months, she attended her weekly CBT session, and found that gradually she could resist her urges to check and count, and saw a significant lowering of her anxiety too.

Acute Stress Reaction (short lived anxiety in response to a specific situation)

This describes the symptoms that people develop after an unexpected traumatic life event, but which tend to be short lived, lasting only a few weeks at most. If the symptoms persist for more than 4–6 weeks, and are increasingly disabling, you may be developing post-traumatic stress disorder, so it is important to discuss your concerns with a healthcare professional, such as a doctor, or with a counsellor or psychologist.

Events that can lead to an acute stress reaction include:

- Bereavement
- Accidents that are life-threatening to yourself or others
- Sexual assault and rape
- Being threatened
- Physical assault
- Domestic violence
- Terrorist incidents
- Road traffic accidents

You may notice yourself feeling anxious, having mood swings, feeling numb or detached from your surroundings, being unable to sleep properly, having flashbacks (unwanted memories) of the event, avoiding places or things that remind you of the event, and the physical sensations associated with "fight or flight" reaction / panic symptoms. You may feel fear, denial, guilt or anger. It is normal for these sensations and emotional ups and downs to occur after a traumatic event, but they should spontaneously settle within days or weeks. If they don't, it is important to seek help quickly.

Initially, after the event, help may be available from friends and family, and it is important to take the time to allow yourself to recover and adjust. Contacting others who were similarly affected may be very supportive.

You might find that talking about it, letting yourself cry, being mindful or resting will help you. Counselling or therapy are options, but most people won't need these for acute stress reactions. Medication to reduce the physical symptoms and reduce the anxiety in the short term may also have a part to play, so please discuss this with your GP.

Real life example

Vinnie was an international student, who had arrived to study just a few days before coming to see the university support team. She was unsure where to get advice. On her way to the airport in a taxi to fly to her new university, she had been involved in a road accident, which had injured her father, and left her with a painful neck. No one had been killed, but she was very shaken up, and had then had to travel on alone. She was feeling quite anxious about her new surroundings and also her neck pain. She had avoided taxis since arriving (the university provided transport for new international students from the airport to their accommodation) and was not sleeping well. She wanted some support and felt like she needed to talk to someone. The support team were able to book her in with a university counsellor, who then talked through her feelings and offered advice and some relaxation activities, as well as suggesting a doctor's appointment for her neck pain. She was offered a follow-up appointment with the counsellor for a week later, and was also advised that more help would be available if her anxiety feelings did not settle within six weeks. She left feeling supported and listened to.

What triggers your anxiety?

Many things can trigger your anxiety. It doesn't have to be events that have already happened; you may be worried about future events, or you may be creating situations in your head.

There are physiological symptoms – the way we feel in our bodies. Your anxiety might be triggered by emotional states or real events, e.g. having to give a talk, or having to work in a group exercise. It might be having to live on your own for the first time. You might find your anxiety spikes when you read your course syllabus and see how much work you've got to do.

There are lots of pressures attached to feeling like you have to always get good grades and keep up with all your social stuff too. So it could be triggered by hearing other students talking about how they're getting on with their assignments or out of class activities. It could be triggered by watching TV because you feel you're not working hard enough or not socialising enough. It could be watching sport and worrying about your own performance. It could be caused by feeling tired, because you haven't had enough sleep, or you had too much to drink the night before.

Your anxiety can even be triggered by imagined events, e.g. imagining how things could have been different in the past, or how things might happen in the future.

Try this for yourself

Think about what triggers your anxiety ...

Are your anxieties in the past or are they future scenarios?

Are they related to people, places, situations, times of day?

Are they physiological – this could be relating to alcohol, caffeine, smoking, lack of sleep, partying too hard?

Does avoidance trigger your anxiety or make you feel more anxious?

Try and monitor your own anxiety in the next couple of weeks and notice what kinds of things trigger it. You might be surprised by what you discover.

Note when you feel anxious in your body or emotionally – it probably means you've encountered a trigger – so have a think about what that could be.

Table 1: Working out my own problematic thoughts, feelings and responses.

When did you last experience your problem?
Where were you? What were you doing?

Describe what happened.

What was going through your head at the time?
What were you thinking? What did you think was the
worst thing that could possibly happen?

How did you feel emotionally?
(Angry / sad / fearful / worried / excited / ashamed, etc.?)

How did you feel in your body?
(Sweaty / blurred vision / stomach turning over /
edgy / keyed up, etc.)

How did you react – what did you do?
Did you avoid anything or seek reassurance from
anyone? (Remember that your reaction can also be a
mental reaction occurring in your head such as a chant,
saying a certain phrase or thought – trying to replace an
unhelpful thought with a neutral or a "good" one.)

What were the consequences of your reaction?
(Even though it might reduce your anxiety immediately,
what are the other consequences of your behaviour?)
For example, I avoided giving a work presentation.

It is four times more common for students to have anxiety AND depression, rather than just one or other of the two conditions
(Bitsika and Sharpley, 2012)

A word about catastrophising – when you fear the worst is going to happen

Sometimes we imagine the worst possible outcome is going to happen, despite there being no reason to suspect that it will. For example, if events in our lives don't go to plan, or we are worried about something, and fear that the worst will happen, this is called catastrophising. Let me give you an example.

Your lecturer passes you in the corridor and quickly calls out, 'Hi, can I catch you later for a quick chat please?'

You fear the worst. But really, this could mean many things. It could be that they want to nominate you for an award, or that they want to ask you to join a project they are overseeing; they might be worried about another student and asking for your help or they could, possibly, be keen to discuss your work.

But in your mind, you have immediately gone to the worst possible scenario – the lecturer is disappointed in your efforts, you are failing the course, and you are going to be asked to leave, or a similar outcome.

Another example might be that you are worried about an exam, but rather than having a healthy concern and a rational approach to the possibility of poor results, and what you might do if you fail, you start to spiral into endless negative scenarios. You imagine all the worst possibilities: you fail the exam, your life takes a disastrous turn, you'll never succeed at anything. You believe you will be a complete "failure".

If you recognise this tendency to magnify ambivalent or difficult situations into something terrible then it may help to address your habit by using some techniques recommended by psychologists, or by speaking to a therapist about it.

CBT techniques work well in these situations, and we'll discuss CBT more, later in the book. But you could start by recognising these thinking patterns, considering the fact that sometimes bad things do happen, then suggesting to yourself some slightly less negative, or even positive outcomes that might happen instead. Talk to trusted friends and family about how you are feeling and be kind to yourself as you try to work on this tricky habit.

CHAPTER 4

ARE WE ALL GETTING MORE ANXIOUS?

There does seem to be a steady increase in the number of young people developing anxiety, according to studies in both the UK and the USA. Around 1 in 4 young women is now thought to be managing a "common mental health" condition, which might include anxiety-related issues (digital. nhs.uk, 2017). For young men the figure is 1 in 10.

> 'I now have no problem with anxiety, it was something I was dealing with in the band ... People saw strength in that, and they didn't seem to expect it from a guy, but they expect it from a female, which to me is crazy. We're all human.'
> **Zayn Malik, singer** (*The Times*, 2017)

Why might the numbers be rising?

It seems fair to say that young people are under pressure like no previous generation. A whole variety of factors are combining to create what can feel like a "pressure cooker society", and it is no surprise therefore that more young people seem to be developing mental health conditions, with anxiety being the most common.

Real life example

Imani was a first-year undergraduate who had recently arrived at university. She was excited to finally start her degree in dentistry but was still kicking herself for "only" getting two A*s and an A, instead of the three A*s she had hoped for, at A level. She was keen to live up to her parents' expectations, and those of her community, who were all so proud of her acceptance to a top university. She was a high achiever, a perfectionist, highly critical of herself when she didn't score top marks or come first, and struggling with the realisation that at university almost everyone around her had also been top of their class and was highly motivated to succeed.

The term had started well enough, but now the assignments were piling up and she was struggling to complete them to her own high standards. She wanted them to be perfect, and when they weren't she would delete them or go over them again and again, but end up handing them in late, which made her anxious too. Talking to other students didn't help as they were also trying to write perfect assignments. She eventually came to the counselling service to ask for help.

The counsellor listened, and then they started to work through what she was trying to achieve, and how perhaps it might be enough to just do *her* best without trying to be *the* best; to be "good enough", (as she clearly was, to have got into dental school) but not try for perfection. Over several sessions they were able to think about these issues, and how Imani's perfectionism had grown over the years, driven by the competitiveness around her and her desire to make her family and friends proud. She realised, after talking with her parents, that they were clearly proud of her, and very supportive of her trying her best, but *they* didn't need her to be top of the class. Imani was able to manage her anxiety and perfectionist traits and it stood her in good stead for the next few years of dental school.

Competitiveness

We have become a society where even the fun stuff has become a competition. Baking cakes, photography, painting, singing and dancing; we now think of these as a type of "competitive sport". Whether it's done by kids at school, or celebrities on TV, we are surrounded worldwide by relentless competition.

And this is particularly true in the university or college lecture hall and tutorial room. The pressure on students is no longer just "to get a broad education" or even just "a degree", but to get a First or top-class qualification, then a post-grad degree, or other diploma. And then the right internship, job offers after university, etc. in a never-ending race to the top, there is at risk of exhausting a whole generation.

Perfectionism

Closely linked to the overly competitive nature of our society is the documented rise in perfectionism among young adults (Curran and Hill, 2017).

The level of universal competitiveness seems to have driven a huge increase in the number of students with perfectionist traits, in the USA, Canada and the UK over the last 30 or so years. With perfectionist traits being closely linked to several mental health conditions, such as anxiety, depression, self-harm, eating disorders and obsessive compulsive disorder, it starts to become apparent why GPs may be seeing more students, like you, who have these conditions.

In trying to keep up with everyone else, trying to be *the* best, not just do *your* best, you may, in some cases, be making yourselves ill.

Social media

So now let's magnify all of that competition and perfectionism with social media.

The lens of Instagram or Snapchat can really pile on the pressure. Not only are students driving themselves harder than ever before, but they are being "monitored" and "graded" 24/7 via their own social media channels.

Social media can be a source of support and useful resources, and may not in itself be causing anxiety in many cases. However, in some cases, it can make a difficult situation worse, and for some, it *will* be the source of anxiety (e.g. seeing traumatic events online). Or it might fuel obsessive tendencies, driving the need for "likes" or followers, or by playing into body image insecurities, making people feel worse. It's important to remember though that social media can also be a source of support and useful resources.

 'Inner peace begins the moment you choose not to allow another event or person to control your emotions.' **Pema Chodron, American Tibetan Buddhist nun**

Other stresses

There are other significant stresses for students, of course, with academic pressure the number one cause of student distress, and, sadly, suicide (hqip.org.uk 2017). This is closely followed by money worries, family issues, health, and relationship difficulties. Other stresses might include bullying, housing issues and workplace issues.

Family and friends, who should be a source of support, can often be a cause of stress, for example, through arguments with flatmates, parental conflict or divorce, parental alcohol or substance use, chronic health conditions in the family or friends' own mental health issues.

Loneliness and isolation

These are relatively new issues for lots of students in a way they perhaps haven't been in the past. Many students are taking to the internet to write blogs about their lonely life. If you often feel isolated, then you are definitely not the only student who feels like this.

Obviously, if you are quite an anxious person that may make it harder for you to meet people. Then if you become isolated, it can make your anxiety worse. So this can be a bit of a vicious cycle, but as you will see there are ways to tackle this.

Some people believe that social media contributes to feelings of isolation and loneliness, as people spend more time on their screens. But others argue that online communities like Twitter allow them to connect with lots of other people who they would never otherwise meet, but who feel the same way as they do, and they support each other.

All these different pressures can really build up at a time of transition and academic expectation. It is therefore unsurprising when some students feel anxious much or all of the time.

 If one or both of your parents suffer from anxiety, there is a higher chance you will too
(Fascinating Facts about Anxiety, 2018)

CHAPTER 5

I THINK I HAVE ANXIETY, WHAT DO I DO NEXT?

At this point in the book, or in life generally, you may be starting to agree that you have anxiety, or something similar, and you may be thinking about next steps.

> 'If you can solve your problem, what need is there to worry? If you can't solve your problem, what is the use of worrying?'
> **Shantideva, 8th century Buddhist monk**

Tell someone

For many people the first thing they do is speak to family or friends about it (Arria et al., 2011). This is a good thing, but not everybody's family or friends always react helpfully or supportively to such conversations or discussions. Sometimes people respond by saying, 'You'll be fine', or 'Just relax!' People don't mean to be unhelpful, but sometimes they just don't know what to say to help you. So it is important to think about what you might do if you don't get the reaction and positive support you were hoping for.

Ask for help

There are many other sources of support for students: healthcare professionals, such as doctors, counsellors and psychologists, counselling and therapy services, online information, university personal tutors, and students' union reps. Some people like to use charity services, and others prefer phone helplines. The good thing is there does seem to be an option for everyone, no matter how shy or anonymous you might wish to be. Book an appointment with your doctor or your student mental health service and start the journey to feeling better.

- Counsellors
- Disability teams
- Doctors and nurses
- Mental health advisors
- Mental health nurses (community psychiatric nurses)
- Psychiatrists
- Psychologists
- Psychological wellbeing practitioners
- University professionals available for mental health support
- Wellbeing advisors

'Worry is like a rocking chair: it gives you something to do but never gets you anywhere.' **Erma Bombeck, American journalist and humourist**

So why doesn't everyone with a mental health or psychological concern seek help?

GPs know that a significant number of people with mental health issues do not seek help. So what about the students who are suffering with anxiety, depression or other symptoms? What is stopping them from approaching any of these people or resources?

Reasons you might not ask for help (Czyz et al., 2013)

- You don't think that you need help or you may not recognise that you have symptoms
- You haven't got time to seek help, and it might interrupt your studies
- You hope that you can sort it out yourself, and don't feel you need professional help
- You fear stigma or discrimination from others
- You stigmatise yourself (i.e. you are harshly critical of yourself for having these issues) (Boerema et al., 2016)
- You don't think you have had the problems for very long
- You worry that other people won't be supportive and understanding
- You lack trust in professionals and worry about confidentiality
- You worry that professionals that you talk to will lack expertise in the topic (Berridge et al., 2017)
- You don't believe in biological or psychological-based explanations for mental health issues (Van Voorhees et al., 2006)
- You have previously experienced poor quality of support or treatment

Let's explore these reasons in a little more detail, as these may be what is standing between you and a healthy, anxiety-free life!

You don't think that you need help or you may not recognise that you have symptoms

One of the most common questions GPs are asked by young people is 'how would I know if I have a mental health problem?' Essentially the answer is that if you don't feel well, if you think something is wrong, if you are not getting the things done that you would expect or need to do, like your work, or meeting people and making friends, or if you are worrying that any of this is happening, then *talk to a professional* to check it out.

You have nothing to lose, and that's what they are there for.

Wellbeing and healthcare professionals, like counsellors and doctors, are trained to ask the right questions, and put it all together. Then they'll share their opinion with you, about whether or not the feelings you are having are, in fact, normal and to be expected, or whether they believe you need additional support or even treatment.

But if you don't feel right, then don't suffer in silence. It is good to talk to friends and family of course, but that may not be quite enough if you are still anxious. So try and talk to someone who has experience in working with mental health problems.

And talking to professionals is confidential.

You haven't got time to seek help and it might interrupt your studies

Maybe this should be looked at the other way round – "you haven't got time to be unwell".

Life is busy, there's no doubt about that, but without your health and, in particular, your psychological health, then it's going to be tough to do all the amazing things you want to do, especially at university. So go on, take five minutes to go online, register with whichever service you want to talk to, and book an appointment. It may be the best thing you do this year.

You hope that you can sort it out yourself, and don't feel you need professional help

Well it is certainly not unreasonable to try and help yourself before seeking professional help, of course, but if you have given it a month or so, using reliable, credible, professionally written resources (see relevant section at end of this book) then it is probably time to run it past a trained counsellor, psychologist or doctor.

There are loads of brilliant self-help options to try, from books to apps to online resources, and being able to say that you tried them first will also show how motivated and engaged you are, so that's a bonus. But everyone needs help sometimes; we are humans, and evolved to be social creatures, so give yourself a break, and allow yourself to be supported by other (compassionate) humans.

You fear stigma or discrimination from others or you stigmatise yourself (i.e. you are harshly critical of yourself for having these issues)

Stigma and discrimination; if it's not other people, then we do it to ourselves. As if life wasn't tough enough, other people criticise us (or we fear that they will) for being human and having emotions, which sometimes get a little overwhelming. The only way to fight this one is to push past their (and sometimes your own) "judge-y" comments (real or imagined) and ask for help anyway. You are worth it.

Other people's opinions may be ill-informed and narrow minded, so you shouldn't value or listen to what they say anyway. You can do this!

You haven't had the problems for very long in your view

If you've had the issues for more than a month, and especially if you've tried to help yourself along the way (see above) then you really shouldn't wait any longer before talking to someone. Life is precious and you shouldn't spend it at the mercy of your mental health issues. There are fantastic and effective treatments out there, so don't spend any more time struggling. Also, you may have to wait on a waiting list for a bit, so best to get signed up and in the queue, if that's the case.

You worry that other people won't be supportive and understanding

It can be difficult to predict how people might react when you tell them you are struggling or need help, but sometimes they will support you and be more understanding and supportive than you might expect. Even if they are less helpful, try not to let that stop you looking after yourself, and getting the help you need. Sometimes the people we care about most are unable to be as fully supportive as we might hope, but that is their issue, not ours. We can only take responsibility for our own lives.

You lack trust in professionals – you worry about confidentiality

Health and wellbeing professionals all work to strict standards of confidentiality, and most have their own professional guidance about keeping information confidential, which they follow carefully. No professional should share your information without discussing this option with you first, and in very limited circumstances, they will consider sharing it if it is in your best interests.

In the rare cases when a professional needs to share your information without your agreement (consent), it would only be if you or someone else was considered to be in immediate (usually life-threatening) danger. They will do their best to seek your consent in these cases too. They cannot share information with future employers, and you will always be asked for your consent before medical information is requested or shared, and that includes for the Armed Forces.

For example, if a person develops a psychotic condition (they lose the ability to recognise that they are ill), and they are likely to hurt themselves or someone else, then a healthcare professional may have to disclose information to keep that person safe, and as mentioned, they will try to obtain consent before doing so. The same would be true in suicidal thinking if a person was considered to be at high risk of severe self-harm.

Students do worry about the sharing of their confidential information, but this is rarely done, certainly not without consent, and only in circumstances where the student themselves will benefit, for example, to plan better therapy or ask for a second, expert opinion.

You worry that professionals that you talk to will lack specialist expertise in the topic

The people who choose to work with students, such as those in university support and health services, do so because they specifically enjoy working with young people, and usually have additional training and expertise in the issues that most commonly affect young adults. For example, half of consultations in university health centres are for a mental health problem (IPPR, 2017), and so the doctors working in these locations tend to have a great deal of experience in managing mental health issues.

They will often work closely with specialist doctors such as psychiatrists, and with psychologists. The university counsellors and wellbeing practitioners are highly trained, and stay up to date with both mandatory and voluntary training programmes and appraisal.

All of these professionals are familiar with the wide variety of mental health issues that affect young people, and have specialist skills to help them manage the students' individual problems. In fact, university support services are probably the most expert teams in caring for student mental health issues.

You don't believe in biological or psychological-based explanations for mental health issues

Some people have a different understanding of emotional difficulties, perhaps believing it to be a spiritual issue, for example. Clearly it is up to each individual to think about their wellbeing in terms that they are comfortable with. It may be helpful to read about mental health on reliable and credible websites (see resources section of this book), or in relevant books, if greater clarity and understanding are desired. But whatever your belief system for explaining mental health issues, there is help available to you.

Many universities have a chaplain, or religious or spiritual leader, for the campus community, who is often linked to local leaders of many faiths and backgrounds, so connecting with them might be a good first step in talking to someone empathic and compassionate, about your anxiety. Chaplains, or other faith leaders, are happy to talk to students of all faiths and those who follow none, and many students find it helpful to talk to someone caring but who is not a healthcare or academic professional at the university, yet who understands campus life. Whatever your beliefs, start the conversation, and see if that helps to relieve some of your worries.

You have previously experienced poor quality of support or treatment

Everyone's experience of care is different, and can depend on a whole variety of factors such as waiting times, reception staff interaction, the attitudes and beliefs of the professional, or treatment side effects or results (benefits and failures). If you have previously encountered poor support or treatment, it's a real shame that it was a negative experience for you. However, the good news is that trying something new or different, or even the same treatment with a different person, can have a different outcome.

Keep an open mind about the type of talking therapy offered, the nature of the therapist, the use of medication, or talking to friends and family about your experiences. Advances in medicine and therapy are made all the time, guidelines are updated, and protocols developed.

What you were offered before may not be what you are offered again. Moving to a new clinical specialist or therapist may be a step change for you, and lead to different, even brilliant, results. It's got to be worth considering, hasn't it?

'You are the one thing in this world, above all other things that you must never give up on. When I was in middle school, I was struggling with severe anxiety and depression and the help and support I received from my family and a therapist saved my life. Asking for help is the first step.' **Lili Reinhart, actress** (Reinhart, 2017)

CHAPTER 6

HELPFUL THINGS THAT PEOPLE DO TO IMPROVE THEIR ANXIETY

The good news is that there are lots of things that you can try to improve your situation before seeing a professional, and many of them are free! Whole websites, blogs and books are dedicated to self-help and relaxation techniques, so have a look and see what works for you.

Here are some more ideas that university GPs recommend you try; they can be really effective:

Relaxation and breathing techniques

Many cultures and religions have recognised for centuries the benefits of focusing on your breathing, being 100% in the current moment and controlling your emotions in that way. Modern versions of meditation include mindfulness, "modern meditation" and colouring (yes, colouring-in pictures). It's not for everyone, but anyone can try, although it may take time to get the hang of it, and feel the benefits of calm descending upon you. The good thing is that there are techniques that can take just a few minutes of your day, but may be beneficial when practised regularly. There are plenty of apps that will talk you through a meditation session (some listed at the end of this book), and count the time for you too. Inner peace may be just an app away ...

> 'If you want to conquer the anxiety of life, live in the moment, live in the breath.'
> **Amit Ray, *OM Chanting and Meditation*** (2010), p.50 – 54

Shifting your attention

The more we give our attention to something, the more powerful that thing becomes. So, a good technique to help us in a stressful situation is being able to shift your attention.

Here's how it works. If you're in a social situation and you're feeling anxious, all your attention will probably be focusing on yourself and how you're feeling. Instead, shift your attention to an external focus – it could be people around you or further away. For example, look at other people's hairstyles and see what you can notice about them. Are their styles long or short, curly or straight, coloured or natural?

You could look to see if people are wearing the same colour – who is wearing the colour blue? Are they wearing blue shoes, blue shirts or carrying a blue bag?

It doesn't have to be with other people – you could do it with inanimate objects. If you're working in the library and you start to feel stressed or anxious about something, try shifting your attention to find 10 red books. Or if you're in a lecture theatre, focus on what's being shown on the screen – are there words and images? What kind of font is it? Is it big or small? It could be the types of door or windows – what shape, colour and size they are. How many are there? Are they the same or different? Try and notice all the little details.

You can shift your attention anywhere, anytime. It is one way to allow yourself to shift outside yourself, so that instead of focusing on your anxiety, you re-focus externally. It can be a useful technique in a test or exam too. As soon as you

start to feel anxious, look down at your desk and notice the corners. Then observe what other right angles you can see – right angles of the computer screen, on the board, on the window, on the paper you're using, and on any posters you can see. It's a very good way of letting your mind re-focus so that you can calm down and get back on track.

Let's try shifting your attention.

Exercise

First, imagine a gremlin ...

This gremlin represents your worry.

Next, focus on this picture of a tree for 20 seconds (you may want to set a timer) and notice everything you can. How many branches does it have? How big or small are the leaves? What shape are the leaves?

What happened after 20 seconds? Were you still thinking about the gremlin?

Hopefully not.

This is a simple example of how refocusing allows you to shift your attention to something else external to your thoughts. Maybe the thought of the gremlin popped back into your head, but hopefully you were able to shift your attention, at least for a second or two.

The next step is replacing that gremlin with something you are actually worried about. It will be harder to shift your focus, but you can do it and it does get easier with practise.

Helpful distraction

While we can't always change the situation we're in, we can choose to distract ourselves – and doing that can help the anxiety to subside and pass. So this is all about finding practical things you can do to be kind to yourself that will help you get over the sense of anxiety and get on with your life.

This is what happens to the anxiety when we use a helpful distraction.

Figure 3: Using helpful distraction.

For some people, putting on their favourite music will help, or going to the gym, or meeting up with friends – find what works best for you. Try and think of some activities that you can do with others, and on your own, outside and inside – because if you are feeling anxious late at night, it might be hard to find other people or do an outside activity.

Try this for yourself

Jot down some ideas here to remind you:

Exercise can make anxiety better, at least temporarily, and potentially in the longer term

Exercise

Scientists have found that regular participation in aerobic exercise has been shown to reduce overall levels of tension, elevate and stabilize mood, improve sleep, and improve self-esteem. About five minutes of aerobic exercise can begin to stimulate anti-anxiety effects.

So says the Anxiety and Depression Association of America in its excellent page on exercise and the benefits on anxiety.

There is overwhelming evidence that exercise, and the release of endorphins, and "using up" of adrenaline, can significantly help people who suffer from anxiety. Whether you take a brisk walk, run, swim or cycle (or choose Ultimate Frisbee!) you can help yourself both emotionally and physically. And it doesn't have to be for long, 10 minutes may be enough if done regularly, with benefits lasting for years if you keep it up. So you will be protecting yourself into the future, as well as getting a bit fitter! Win-win!

 'Promised myself I would not let exercise be the first thing to go by the wayside when I got busy ... and here is why: it has helped me with my anxiety in ways I've never dreamed possible. To those struggling with anxiety, OCD, depression: I know it's mad annoying when people tell you to exercise, and it took me about 16 medicated years to listen. I'm glad I did.' **Lena Dunham, actress, writer** (Dunham, 2015)

Reduce caffeine

Caffeine is a well-known stimulant, both of the brain and the heart. It raises our blood pressure, but it also raises our levels of adrenaline, noradrenaline and cortisol (our "stress hormones"). And we don't develop tolerance to these effects either, so the fact that we regularly down caffeine-containing drinks does not reduce the likelihood of these effects on our wellbeing (Lane et al., 1990).

Caffeine essentially magnifies the "fight or flight" reaction, causing us to feel on edge and jittery, which, if you are already prone to anxiety, is especially unhelpful.

And, of course, caffeine will stop you getting a good night's sleep, which will just make your anxiety worse too, so that's another reason to go easy on the lattes and other caffeinated drinks!

Journaling

Writing a journal has become increasingly popular as a way to reflect on our emotions. It can be very therapeutic to sit and write down your thoughts, look at what may have upset you that day, how you managed it, and what you might do differently another time.

Also writing down all the *positive* things that happened, and taking the time to congratulate yourself on what you did well, can be very rewarding, as can feeling gratitude for the good things in your life (Niles et al., 2013).

Nature

Spending time in nature is well recognised as being of great help to good mental health. Anxiety and depression have both been shown to be reduced by time spent outdoors, whether it's an hour-long daily walk, or half an hour a week strolling in the local park, (Bratman et al., 2015) it's all good for us. Road cycling, outdoor boxercise and mountain biking have also been found to be of benefit (Mackay and Neill, 2010).

The big message here is – it's good to feel the wind in your hair and be out in the elements sometimes!

 Re-labelling anxiety as being "excited" may help you perform better (Heysigmund.com, 2018)

CHAPTER 7

UNHELPFUL THINGS THAT PEOPLE TRY TO IMPROVE THEIR ANXIETY

Historically, anxiety has been treated with some pretty horrible methods and medicines over the centuries, even up until 20 years ago, which might explain why some people are still worried about seeking help now. The good news is that these days, treatment options are acceptable and generally successful.

This "historical hangover" however, of avoiding seeking professional help, has led to an understandable amount of public experimentation in *self-medication*.

In other words, it has become common for people to use alcohol, and sometimes a variety of chemical substances varying from prescription pills to "weed" (cannabis), to try to control or reduce their anxiety.

Safety behaviours

Sometimes people engage in "safe" behaviours which, they think will prevent, stop or minimise their anxiety. This could be as simple as thinking *every time I have a bad thought, I will replace it with a good one*. Or it could involve a compulsion, such as counting in threes until the bad thought disappears or attempting to undo or neutralise the unpleasant thought in some other way. That might sound harmless, but actually, every time the person does a safety behaviour, they're taking the fear or worry to be true, or believing that it is likely to be true, thus reinforcing the fear and making it stronger.

Alcohol

For some people, the reason they first seek professional help is actually for their alcohol use, rather than for the underlying anxiety, and unfortunately this is not always recognised by the counsellor or doctor that they speak to. The healthcare or welfare professional may then focus on the alcohol use, but omit to ask about the underlying reasons for its use, and so overlook the anxiety disorder that needs help.

It may be worth taking a moment to think about whether you drink more, for example, to help you relax in social situations or at parties, to help you to sleep or even to help you relax in the workplace / academic environment. These are all common ways that students try to cope and use alcohol, when their anxiety is stopping them from doing the things they need or want to be doing, such as meeting new people, hanging out with friends, studying or sleeping.

Cannabis

Cannabis is another popular self-medication option, despite the fact that cannabis can have mixed effects, depending on the person. For some it creates a calm feeling, but for others it will make them feel sick, and their heart will race, thus making the anxiety worse. A bigger issue may be the fact that it can create dependence (addiction), and in the longer term, regular use may lead to issues with worsening mental health, depression, anxiety, memory problems, and possibly psychosis ("cannabis-induced psychosis"). Cannabis-induced psychosis is a real and increasing risk. And its symptoms tend to be of erratic moods, paranoia, poor concentration, poor memory and rising anxiety (Grewal and George, 2017). It is well worth being aware of these risks when considering your options, even if you have used it without issues in the past. Problems with cannabis use can occur at any time regardless of how much cannabis you have used in the past.

Prescription medication (without a prescription)

It's also not uncommon for students to buy medications online, without a prescription, to help them to relax. It is worth knowing that it is illegal for UK-based websites to sell prescription-only medications, such a diazepam or antidepressants, without a prescription. It is also illegal in the UK for you to possess certain medications (such as benzodiazepines as they are Class C controlled drugs), if they have not been prescribed for you.

You may assume that because these are prescription-only medications that they will somehow be "safer". Unfortunately, this is not the case and such medications are often highly addictive, such as Valium (diazepam), or dangerous if not taken as prescribed by a professional, for example, because of the risk of accidental overdose. Healthcare professionals are of course also prescribing specifically for you, with your medical history, knowing your physiology, what other medications you take, and with your family history in mind.

Taking prescription medications without medical guidance is a high-risk strategy.

There has been a rise in the number of people seeking help for dependence on prescription pills in the UK, with clinics now being set up specifically to help those addicted to online, illicitly bought prescription medications. Many of those now asking for and seeking help originally started the pills to self-medicate their anxiety, or they were prescribed them by a doctor, but then were unable to get them on repeat prescription because of their addictive nature. They are now stuck in a tricky cycle of needing medication for anxiety, but unable to get it in a legitimate manner. The clinics are supporting them, but recovery from addition will take time.

A whole variety of short acting drugs are available, such as benzodiazepines ("-zepam" or "-zolam" drugs e.g. Xanax – alprazolam), but these are not a problem-free solution, even if they are effective for some. Their biggest risks are addiction, or overdosing.

Beta blocker ("-olol") medications are another short acting option, and safer in many ways, working mainly to block the physical symptoms of the fight or flight reaction, and not having addictive properties. They can seem attractive to source online but this really isn't a good idea. They are prescription-only medications, like benzodiazepines, and could potentially have harmful side effects if a doctor hasn't checked that they are suitable for you, with full knowledge of your medical history and family medical background.

There are other medications for anxiety, that a few people might try taking without prescription, but this is rarer, these will be discussed when we look at medication under treatment options for anxiety.

 Anxiety can confuse your sense of smell, making neutral smells smell bad!
(Krusemark et al., 2013)

CHAPTER 8

TALKING AND PSYCHOLOGICAL THERAPY

For each of the anxiety-related conditions there are slightly different recommended talking and psychological treatments, in terms of type and duration, based on CBT principles. But essentially all anxiety disorders respond well to talking therapies, so it is always worth exploring these options first, especially as they are unlikely to have negative effects, such as side effects or interactions, in the way that medicines might.

Many people need talking therapies and tablets to help their anxiety, as one or the other is not quite enough. If you have tried one without the other and not had a positive outcome, it may be because you need a combination of both medicine and CBT to get better. This is fine, and there is more information on medicines in the next chapter.

How do I find a therapist?

To find local free NHS talking therapy, look up *"NHS talking therapies near me"* online, as you may be able to refer yourself directly, without seeing a doctor. This means you could book yourself straight into a group or individual therapy for free, online.

If you prefer a private CBT trained therapist in the UK (you will pay a fee), search the (BABCP British Association of Behaviour and Cognitive Psychotherapies).

Which therapy?

If we remind ourselves about our Anxiety Umbrella (below) we can then take a look and see which therapies or treatments are currently recommended for each of the conditions below it, remembering that availability may vary slightly from area to area, but the principles of evidence-based therapy will stay the same.

This should then help you to have an informed discussion with the therapist, or healthcare professional assessing you, and to read about it in advance of any session if you wish to. Therapy is not "passive" and you will need to be engaged and keen to get the most from it.

PHOBIAS
Panic Disorder
ACUTE STRESS REACTION
Social Anxiety Disorder
Generalised Anxiety Disorder
OBSESSIVE COMPULSIVE DISORDER

You don't have to do any preparation of course, but this is just for information in case you want to know more (pathways.nice.org.uk, 2018). More detailed information about the talking therapies themselves is in the boxes.

On the next page is a brief summary (for quick reference) of the recommended treatments for the different conditions.

Please note that the information provided on session length and duration of treatment are just recommended guidelines. Each individual case may require more or fewer sessions, and the length of sessions may vary.

Phobias

Recommended talking therapy for most phobias, is CBT specifically the Clark and Wells or Heimberg model. That may or may not involve exposure therapy.

Many people with phobias may not need formal treatments though, and may cope well using self-help CBT techniques.

Recommended duration: (depending on the severity of the phobia) around 12 sessions

Intervals: weekly, up to one hour per session

Social Anxiety Disorder

Recommended talking therapy: CBT specifically the Clark and Wells or Heimberg model. Group work has not been found to be successful for people with social anxiety, as they may be too anxious about being around other people to get enough from the sessions.

Recommended duration: 16.5–21 hours total

Intervals: weekly, up to 90 mins per session

Generalised Anxiety Disorder

Recommended talking therapy: group work first, then individual (one-to-one) CBT (Cognitive Behavioural Therapy) if group work is not helpful, or Applied Relaxation (AR – see notes in box) as an alternative to CBT.

Recommended duration: 12–15 hours total CBT or AR

Intervals: weekly, one hour long

Panic Disorder

Recommended talking therapy: CBT

Recommended duration: 7–14 hours total

Intervals: weekly, one hour long

Obsessive Compulsive Disorder

Recommended talking therapy: CBT including Exposure and Response Prevention (ERP) for some people with compulsive behaviours, in particular.

Recommended duration: 10 hours minimum

Intervals: weekly, one hour long

Acute Stress Reaction

People who have suffered an acute trauma or shock should *not* receive brief single sessions for "debriefing" or talking about the incident. This has not been shown to be helpful and may in fact make things worse.

In young people, if symptoms are still there after a month, a treatment called trauma-focused CBT (five sessions) may be helpful. If the symptoms are still there after three months and PTSD (post-traumatic stress disorder) is likely, then other specialised therapies such as EMDR (Eye Movement Desensitisation and Reprocessing), or, again, trauma-focused CBT, may be effective. Such treatments are likely to take several months to complete (8–12 sessions in total).

If other mental health conditions are present alongside your anxiety, for example depression, the therapist will work with you to decide how best to approach treatment, which condition to tackle first and together you can make a plan for recovery. CBT is usually helpful for most of these anxiety and depressive conditions.

What is Cognitive Behavioural Therapy (CBT)?

We've talked a bit about CBT. So let's take a closer look at how it can help. The aim of CBT is to change the way we respond or behave in response to what we are thinking and feeling.

CBT is a really effective approach for anxiety issues. It looks at the links between the events in our lives, how we interpret those events, and our responses to them.

Cognitions are the ways we think, what we believe, and how we interpret things. The way we feel is our emotional response to these things. And our behaviours are what we do in response to them, mentally or physically.

For example, *I am a failure* as a thought (cognition) leads us to feel sad, numb and unable to do the things we want to do. This leads us to think we are even more of a "failure" (this reinforces the negative thoughts), and so it becomes a vicious cycle. This is sometimes called a "negative thought spiral".

CBT tries to break this cycle by training our minds to have a *new* reaction to negative thoughts, and eventually to change the negative thoughts.

If we change our thoughts, we can change our reactions and our behaviours. And our difficult emotions will also change, or at least decrease in severity or intensity.

It may also work on tackling challenging situations we find ourselves in, or physical symptoms in response to stress.

It is *not* a quick fix, and you may have to work hard, by keeping a note of feelings, thoughts and actions between sessions. Your therapist will help you with this. It is a present-focused therapy, and will equip you with all the skills and strategies you need to help yourself, now and in the future.

It focuses on the present, not the past.

Here are some very common thinking problems – these are some of the most common things that people have.

Catastrophising Thinking the worst-case scenario about every event, no matter how minor.

Black and white thinking Experiences or things are only categorised as one way or another, often as good or bad, with no in-between.

Crystal ball thinking Thinking you can predict the future, or living as if the future has happened.

Jumping to conclusions Making a judgement, usually negative, even when there is little or no evidence for it.

Magnified duty Believing you are 100 per cent responsible or have an increased responsibility for things, discounting the fact that other people may share responsibility.

Personalising Thinking that everything is your fault, even when you couldn't have had anything to do with it.

"Should be" and "ought to be" Thinking things HAVE to be a certain way, or people (including you) SHOULD behave in a particular way.

Emotional reasoning Basing things on how you feel, rather than reality.

Overestimation of likelihood Believing an event to be imminent and extremely likely to take place despite how unlikely it is in reality.

Mind reading Believing that you know what other people are thinking, despite having no evidence for it.

What is Exposure Therapy?

CBT for anxiety problems will include exposure therapy, or Exposure and Response Prevention (ERP) in the case of obsessional problems. During exposure therapy a person repeatedly puts themselves in the situation that creates anxiety for them, for example, social situations. It is done in a measured and controlled way, to help retrain the brain, so that it stops sending out "fight or flight" panic messages to the body in situations where it is unhelpful and unnecessary, giving people more helpful and accurate ways of thinking about fearful situations.

Repeated exposure, or contact, with the thing that makes you very anxious e.g. being on the Underground, will gradually allow your brain and body to stop overreacting to this trigger, and you will be able to cope much better in such circumstances.

What is Applied Relaxation?

This is a relaxation and breathing technique that people can learn to counteract feelings of anxiety, and is recommended specifically for people suffering from general anxiety disorder, to allow them to be able to relax in stressful situations. They gradually learn the relaxation techniques over several weeks, and these include progressively relaxing the different muscles of the body, leading to a less dramatic reaction when they feel anxious.

Try this for yourself

Progressive muscle relaxation

This is a great way to relieve tension in the body, helping you to re-focus when you need to.

1) Sit in a comfortable position and close your eyes. Take some deep breaths. Expand your belly as you breathe in. Contract it as you breathe out.

2) Start with your head. Tense your facial muscles, and squeeze those eyes shut. Clench your your jaw, hold it, then release. Keep those deep breaths coming in and out.

3) Life your shoulders up to your ears. Hold, then release and breathe.

4) Make a fist with your right hand. Tighten the muscles in your lower and upper arm, then hold and release. Breathe in and out. Repeat the routine with your left hand.

5) Next, concentrate on your back. Squeeze your shoulder blades together. Hold, then release. Breathe in and out.

6) Suck your stomach in, hold, then release. Breathe in and out.

7) Clench your buttocks, hold, then release. Breathe in and out. Breathe in and out. Repeat with left hamstring.

8) Tighten your right hamstring, hold, then release. Breathe in and out. Repeat with left hamstring.

9) Flex your right calf, hold, then release. Breathe in and out. Repeat with left calf.

10) Tighten toes on your right foot, hold, then release. Breathe in and out. Repeat this with your left foot.

As mentioned in Chapter 6, two other strategies that can be useful in trying to manage yourself in stressful or anxiety provoking situations are "shifting your attention" and "helpful distraction".

Shifting your attention to external or non-threatening things can help alleviate your anxiety quickly and allow you to refocus.

Helpful distraction is a way of allowing the anxiety to pass without having to actively avoid it (which we know is not a good way to deal with anxiety problems). It is choosing to do something different whilst waiting for the anxiety to subside – which it always will.

CHAPTER 9

PILLS, PILLS, PILLS!

Whether you call them pills, tablets, medicines, drugs or medication, the pharmacological approach to treatment for anxiety can transform the lives of many students with anxiety.

> Medication can reduce anxiety, and in some cases is as effective as talking therapy or CBT. It is often used in conjunction with talking therapy or CBT for best treatment effects.

So why do people worry about medication?

A lot of people worry about taking medication for their mental health, yet they would never argue with the idea of someone taking insulin for diabetes, or an inhaler for asthma.

Medication is acceptable for most physical conditions, but we still have a long way to go with destigmatising and understanding mental health treatments.

A few wellbeing and psychological practitioners may be unduly reluctant to support their clients taking medicines, though there are safe, evidence-based and effective treatments available. This can make it difficult for students to seek help, and discuss their medications with their counsellors or other therapists, fearing that they will be challenged for needing to take medication. Hopefully this won't happen, but it may be the case that professionals, whether other doctors, nurses or psychologists, may not always hold the same views on treatment!

We don't yet understand neurobiology (brain science) well enough to know whether or not those with anxiety also have a fundamental "biochemical deficiency" like diabetics do, so perhaps we should stay open minded about treatments that might help them, how they work exactly, and what you may find effective.

Medication is undoubtedly effective and safe for many people with anxiety, so let's take a look at what you might be offered. Some studies (Bandelow et al., 2015) are now showing that medication may be even *more* effective than talking therapies, such as CBT alone, so pills are certainly worth a look, although they may have side effects and interactions, of course. The evidence seems to be that psychological techniques plus medication is most effective for moderate to severe anxiety.

Things to remember about medication

Stay open minded about medication

Many students worry about seeing a GP because they might be offered medication and feel pressured to take it, but it would in fact be wrong of GPs *not* to consider this option if it might help, and therefore they should at least offer it, and discuss all options with their patient. People don't have to take the medication if they don't want to.

The student is then able to say 'no thank you' if they wish, having had an informed discussion, while keeping an open mind for the future if possible, in case things deteriorate and their situation changes.

So the thing to remember here is that GPs are *supposed* to offer their patients a full and informed discussion about **all** treatment options, including medication, so that you can make your own decision about what you would like to try. Don't avoid a visit to the GP because they will mention medication; that's the right thing for them to do, so you can hear all your options, before making your decision.

You are the boss

University GPs will generally say to student before they try new mediation, 'If you don't like taking them, and it's been less than eight weeks, just stop. You are in control. But try them with an open mind, they might be helpful ...'

Students often worry about becoming addicted, but it may be reassuring to know that GPs are generally very careful, and take the time to explain about the level of risk of addiction with different tablets (only a few have addictive possibilities), as well as talking about potential side effects. GPs should monitor these, and your progress, carefully, with regular reviews to check for any side effects, and to make sure the medications are helping, not making things worse.

What if there are problems with the tablets?

If you ever have problems with the medication before your next appointment is due and you feel the problems can't wait, then call and leave a message for the GP to contact you. Doctors are there to help you, and want to know if things are not going well and need urgent review.

And finally ...

GPs will tell you that they have lost count of the number of students who eventually try medication and at their review appointment 2–4 weeks later say, 'I wish I'd tried these sooner! I'm not sure why I was so worried about taking medication'. Medication really can transform things, often within a month or two, and get you back on track, and then later on you can stop them at the right time, gradually, and in discussion with your doctor.

Real life example

Jon came to see the doctor out of desperation. He was a final year PhD student, and barely sleeping. He had struggled for years with poor sleep, and this had slowly worn him down, interfering with his ability to work, and causing him to feel anxious about completing his PhD on time. Deadlines were looming and he didn't know where to turn. Over the years he had tried various things to help his sleep, which worked a bit, but now the anxiety was keeping him awake too, and disrupting his concentration in the daytime. He had tried mindfulness and talking therapies, but nothing was really helping at this point. He asked the doctor about medication as a "last resort" and they discussed his options. There was indeed a medication which he could try taking at night, which would help both his sleep and his anxiety. It might have side effects initially, but these would wear off quite quickly. He planned to come back in 10 days to see the doctor and discuss his progress, or any problems. Ten days later Jon was back. He was delighted with how both his sleep and his anxiety had improved. He had indeed felt groggy in the day time for a week or so but that had now settled and he was working normally, focused and productive. He said he couldn't believe the difference and that this option of tablets had never been mentioned before. He knew it wasn't a long-term solution, but for now, with the PhD his priority, he could finish his work and then look to the future for longer-term ways to manage his sleep issues and anxiety. Medication had been the right option for him at that time.

What prescription medications are used for anxiety?

A variety of medicines can be prescribed (MedicinesComplete, 2018).

Short term

- Some types (variously called anxiolytics, hypnotics, sedatives and tranquilisers) relax you, and may make you sleepy at a certain dose.
- These can be addictive (if taken regularly for 2–4 weeks or more) and are for short-term use only, such as for sudden onset, severe and disabling anxiety.
- They include benzodiazepines such as diazepam, temazepam or lorazepam.
- They are sometimes prescribed to take alongside a new antidepressant, e.g. an SSRI (see below), as these can make anxiety slightly worse before it gets better, so the benzodiazepines balance this out.

Long term

- Antidepressants, in particular SSRIs (Serotonin Selective Reuptake Inhibitors), for example, citalopram or sertraline, and SNRIs (Serotonin and Noradrenaline Reuptake Inhibitors) such as venlafaxine or duloxetine, are all (at specific doses) effective for anxiety, not just depression.
- These are not addictive, and tend to be for longer-term anxiety issues such as OCD, social anxiety disorder, PTSD and generalised anxiety disorder, alongside talking therapy.
- They are generally well tolerated, but should not be stopped suddenly once people have been taking them for more than about eight weeks, so withdrawal after this should be tapered slowly over a few weeks.

- If you do stop suddenly the withdrawal effects include dizziness, insomnia and flu-like symptoms (muscle pains).
- Their side effects might include sleep disturbance, nausea, diarrhoea, headaches and dizziness, and they can make anxiety worse when you start them, so many doctors will also offer a short-term medication to be taken alongside the antidepressant for the first few days, such as a benzodiazepine, to balance this effect.
- Side effects may last a week or two, so to minimise the possibility of suffering from them, it is a good idea to take only half of the normal prescribed dose for the first week or 10 days.

For physical symptoms

- There are also medications which block the physical (bodily) effects of anxiety, such as beta blockers e.g. propranolol, but these have no effect on the brain or our thinking.
- These can be useful for short-term situations such as exams, driving tests or presentations in front of a crowd.
- Beta blockers can have occasional side effects such as dizziness, tiredness or diarrhoea, but are generally well tolerated.

Rarer medicines

- Buspirone is rarely used in the UK, and is used for short-term anxiety only.
- Clomipramine / imipramine can be used as a second line medication for panic disorder and obsessive compulsive disorder, but tend to cause many more side effects than modern medications. These can include dry mouth, constipation, drowsiness, blurred vision and irregular heartbeat.
- Pregabalin tends to be used when other medication has not worked for generalised anxiety disorder.

CHAPTER 10

IN SUMMARY

It may be helpful at this point, before we look at where you can find out more, to recap some of the key points about anxiety in case you are struggling, or know someone who is.

Facts

- Anxiety is extremely common, and affects more women than men.
- Anxiety often occurs with other mental health or developmental problems, such as depression, ADHD or Asperger's.
- Having certain physical problems makes anxiety more likely to be an issue, for example irritable bowel syndrome, migraines, and pain-related conditions.
- The longer you leave it, the harder it might be to sort out, so ask for help from a counsellor, psychologist or doctor, and start some sort of treatment as soon as you can – don't delay!
- People develop many unhelpful ways of dealing with anxiety, including avoidance and safety behaviours, which ironically make the anxiety worse rather than resolving it.
- You don't need to be perfect; just try your best, you don't have to be the best! Remeber perfectionism is associated with high levels of anxiety.

- Alcohol and drugs are commonly used to try to cope with anxiety but will make things worse in the long run, so seek help ASAP if you think you might be doing this.
- People will always find reasons not to get help and change things, but you *can* do this: take back control of your life and do the things you want to do, by dealing with your anxiety, not ignoring it.

Getting help

- Try the resources in the next section to learn more about anxiety, or to hear from people who have experienced it and can share their thoughts on how best to manage it.
- Talk to family or friends for everyday support.
- There are lots of self-help options for anxiety: relaxation techniques, mindfulness and breathing techniques, so start with these to see if you can take helpful steps for yourself. You'll feel good for trying, and there's always more help if you are struggling.
- Your university will provide free help, for example in the counselling or wellbeing services.
- Every UK university has a free counselling service.
- Look at your university **student support** services website as a first step to see what they can offer, or your university doctor's practice (GP surgery).
- Many universities offer online support too, so that's another option to consider if you aren't keen to talk face-to-face yet.
- NHS talking therapies are provided free, look up "NHS talking therapies near me" online.

Therapy options

- Lots of help is available, both through talking therapies or medicines.
- The main thing is to take the first step and talk to a professional about your options.

- No one will make you do anything you don't want to do.
- Services are confidential, so you can speak freely and share your worries.
- CBT will almost always be the first line treatment you are offered where available: this will involve a course of talking sessions.
- You may be offered group sessions, which can be a good first step for many conditions (though not social anxiety disorder).
- If you try the talking therapy and it is not working even after a recommended amount of time, or your symptoms are severe and disabling, you may be offered tablets (medication) to help the talking therapy to work better.
- Medication can work very well and effectively for many anxiety conditions, and there are both short- and long-term types to try, depending on your problems.
- A doctor will be happy to discuss your personal situation and come to a decision with you about which medicine may be worth trying, as well as discussing potential side effects, how long to take them for, and any other concerns you may have.
- They should then review you regularly to check all is going well.

Try this for yourself

Your action plan

What do you want to do after reading this book that might help you manage your anxiety?

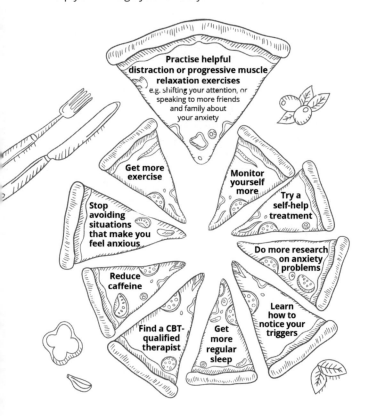

Practise helpful distraction or progressive muscle relaxation exercises e.g. shifting your attention, or speaking to more friends and family about your anxiety

Get more exercise

Monitor yourself more

Try a self-help treatment

Stop avoiding situations that make you feel anxious

Do more research on anxiety problems

Reduce caffeine

Learn how to notice your triggers

Find a CBT-qualified therapist

Get more regular sleep

See a GP to discuss medication options in line with how you're feeling.

Please remember ...

If you are struggling with your wellbeing it is vital to let your university know what is happening for you, to make sure that you receive the right support and to ensure fairness in any assessment they make of you and your work.

Every university will have a process for what are called "mitigating" or "extenuating" circumstances (special circumstances that may impact on your academic performance, including physical and mental health issues, bereavement, and other significant life events).

These can happen to anyone, so make sure that you let the university know: talk to your tutor, complete the necessary forms and get the support you need and deserve.

CHAPTER 11

WHERE CAN I FIND OUT MORE?

Books

- *OCD, Anxiety, Panic Attacks and Related Depression: The Definitive Survival and Recovery Approach* by Adam Shaw and Lauren Callaghan

- *Overcoming Anxiety* by Helen Kennerley (recommended by the NHS, a self-help guide, with CBT techniques to help you deal with your anxiety yourself)

- *How to Survive the End of the World (when it's in your own head); an anxiety survival guide* by Aaron Gillies (@ TechnicallyRon) (a chatty and honest account of his own anxiety and what he has found helpful, along with interviews of others who have also managed their anxiety)

- *Notes on a Nervous Planet* by Matt Haig (a best-selling view of what is making us all anxious, and his own anxiety, in the 21st century)

- *Overcome Social Anxiety and Shyness: A Step-by-Step Self-Help Action Plan to Overcome Social Anxiety, Defeat Shyness and Create Confidence* by Dr Matt Lewis (a step-by-step workbook for those with social anxiety, helping them to build confidence in bite sized chunks)

- *We're All Mad Here* by Claire Eastham (blogger turns writer to explain what has helped her manage her social anxiety, in a no holds barred account)

- *How to Deal with OCD: A 5-step, CBT-based plan for overcoming obsessive compulsive disorder* by Dr Elizabeth Forrester (short, easy to read, self-help based on CBT for tackling your OCD symptoms)
- *The OCD Workbook: your guide to breaking free from obsessive compulsive disorder (3rd Ed)* by C Pedrick and B Hyman (a workbook used in hospitals too, for you to work though, for OCD and also hair picking or body dysmorphic disorder)
- *Manage Your Mind: the Mental Fitness Guide* by G Butler and T Hope (a general support guide for building our skills in resilience, self-esteem and self-confidence)

Websites (some with helplines)

- Young Minds **www.youngminds.org.uk**
- Anxiety UK **www.anxietyuk.org.uk**
- British Association of Counselling and Psychotherapy **www.bacp.co.uk**
- British Association of Behavioural and Cognitive Psychotherapies **www.babcp.com**
- Samaritans **www.samaritans.org**
- Stonewall (for LGBT support) **www.youngstonewall.org.uk**
- Mermaids (for Gender issues) **www.mermaidsuk.org.uk**
- (Support for Sleep) **https://youngminds.org.uk/find-help/feelings-and-symptoms/sleep-problems/**
- Student Minds **www.studentminds.org.uk**
- No Panic **www.nopanic.org.uk**
- Anxiety and Depression Association of America **https://adaa.org**
- OCD UK **www.ocduk.org**
- OCD Action **www.ocdaction.org.uk**
- Triumph over Phobia **www.triumphoverphobia.com**

Apps

- *Self-Help for Anxiety Management (SAM)* app (free) **sam-app.org.uk**
- *Student Health* App (free) **www.expertselfcare. com/ health-apps/student-health-app/**
- *Headspace* for guided meditation app (paid) **www.headspace.com/headspace-meditation-app**
- *Calm* app for meditation (free trial, but paid) **www.calm.com**
- *Colorfy* app for mindful colouring (free) **www.colorfy.net**
- *Aura* app for meditation (free option but pay for more) **www.aurahealth.io**

TED Talks

- How to Make Stress Your Friend by Kelly McGonigal
- How to end stress, anxiety and unhappiness to live in a beautiful state by Preetha Ji
- Be the warrior not the worrier by Angela Ceberano
- How to cope with Anxiety by Olivia Remes
- Surviving Anxiety by Salome Tibebu
- What I learnt from 78,000 GP consultations with university students by Dr Dominique Thompson

YouTube

- Pooky Knightsmith on Mental Health; multiple useful short videos

REFERENCES

8 Fascinating Facts About Anxiety: Symptoms, a. (2018). *8 Fascinating Facts About Anxiety*. [online] Neurocore. Available at: www.neurocorecenters.com/8-facts-anxiety-symptoms-statistics#cOg27L67E8PUBD5S.97 [Accessed 30 Jul. 2018].

Adaa.org. (2018). *Facts & Statistics | Anxiety and Depression Association of America, ADAA*. [online] Available at: adaa.org/about-adaa/press-room/facts-statistics [Accessed 30 Jul. 2018].

Anxiety UK. (2018). *Generalised Anxiety Disorder – Anxiety UK*. [online] Available at: www.anxietyuk.org.uk/anxiety-type/generalised-anxiety-disorder/ [Accessed 29 Jul. 2018].

Arria, A., Winick, E., Garnier-Dykstra, L., Vincent, K., Caldeira, K., Wilcox, H. and O'Grady, K. (2011). Help Seeking and Mental Health Service Utilization Among College Students With a History of Suicide Ideation. *Psychiatric Services*, [online] 62(12), pp.1510–13. Available at: www.ncbi.nlm.nih.gov/pubmed/22193801 [Accessed 1 Aug. 2018].

Babcp.com. (2018). *BABCP | British Association for Behavioural & Cognitive Psychotherapies*. [online] Available at: www.babcp.com [Accessed 15 Aug. 2018].

Baldwin, D., Anderson, I., Nutt, D., Allgulander, C., Bandelow, B., den Boer, J., Christmas, D., Davies, S., Fineberg, N., Lidbetter, N., Malizia, A., McCrone, P., Nabarro, D., O'Neill, C., Scott, J., van der Wee, N. and Wittchen, H. (2014). Evidence-based pharmacological treatment of anxiety disorders, post-traumatic stress disorder and obsessive-compulsive disorder: A revision of the 2005 guidelines from the British Association for Psychopharmacology. *Journal of Psychopharmacology*, [online] 28(5), pp.403–39. Available at: www.ncbi.nlm.nih.gov/pubmed/24713617 [Accessed 7 Aug. 2018].

Bandelow, B., Reitt, M., Röver, C., Michaelis, S., Görlich, Y. and Wedekind, D. (2015). Efficacy of treatments for anxiety disorders. *International Clinical Psychopharmacology*, [online] 30(4), pp.183–92. Available at: www.ncbi.nlm.nih.gov/pubmed/25932596 [Accessed 7 Aug. 2018].

Berridge, B. (2017). *Perceived Barriers and Enablers of Help-Seeking for Substance Use Problems During Adolescence - Bonita J. Berridge, Terence V. McCann, Ali Cheetham, Dan I. Lubman*, 2018. [online] Journals.sagepub.com. Available at: http://journals.sagepub.com/doi/abs/10.1177/1524839917691944 [Accessed 1 Aug. 2018].

Bitsika, V. and Sharpley, C. (2012). Comorbidity of anxiety-depression among Australian university students: implications for student counsellors. *British Journal of Guidance & Counselling*, [online] 40(4), pp.385–94. Available at: https://bmcpsychiatry.biomedcentral.com/articles/10.1186/s12888-016-079 0-0 [Accessed 1 Aug 2018].

Boerema, A., Kleiboer, A., Beekman, A., van Zoonen, K., Dijkshoorn, H. and Cuijpers, P. (2016). Determinants of help-seeking behavior in depression: a cross-sectional study. *BMC Psychiatry*, [online] 16(1). Available at: https://bmcpsychiatry.biomedcentral.com/articles/10.1186/s12888-016-0790-0 [Accessed 1 Aug. 2018].

Bratman, G., Daily, G., Levy, B. and Gross, J. (2015). The benefits of nature experience: Improved affect and cognition. *Landscape and Urban Planning*, [online] 138, pp.41–50. Available at: www.sciencedirect.com/science/article/pii/S0169204615000286 [Accessed 18 Sep. 2018].

Chris Fraley, R., Niedenthal, P., Marks, M., Brumbaugh, C. and Vicary, A. (2006). Adult Attachment and the Perception of Emotional Expressions: Probing the Hyperactivating Strategies Underlying Anxious Attachment. *Journal of Personality*, [online] 74(4), pp.1163–90. Available at: https://onlinelibrary.wiley.com/doi/abs/10.1111/j.1467-6494.2006.00406.x [Accessed 18 Sep. 2018].

Curran, T. and Hill, A. (2017). Perfectionism is increasing over time: A meta-analysis of birth cohort differences from 1989 to 2016. *Psychological Bulletin*.

Czyz, E., Horwitz, A., Eisenberg, D., Kramer, A. and King, C. (2013). Self-reported Barriers to Professional Help Seeking Among College Students at Elevated Risk for Suicide. *Journal of American College Health*, [online] 61(7), pp.398–406. Available at: www.ncbi.nlm.nih.gov/pubmed/24010494 [Accessed 1 Aug. 2018].

Dray, K. (2017). *Adele emotionally explains why she may never tour again*. [online] Stylist. Available at: www.stylist.co.uk/people/adele-panic-attack-anxiety-why-never-tour-again-concert-tickets/33141 [Accessed 23 Jan. 2019].

Dunham, L. (2015). *Lena Dunham on Instagram: "Promised myself I would not let exercise be the first thing to go by the wayside when I got busy with Girls Season 5 and here is why: it…"*. [online] Instagram. Available at: www.instagram.com/p/1WoYh8C1GY/ [Accessed 23 Jan. 2019].

El-Gabalawy, R., Mackenzie, C., Shooshtari, S. and Sareen, J. (2011). Comorbid physical health conditions and anxiety disorders: a population-based exploration of prevalence and health outcomes among older adults. *General Hospital Psychiatry*, [online] 33(6), pp.556–64. Available at: https://s3.amazonaws.com/academia.edu.documents/45181825/Comorbid_physical_health_conditions_and_20160428-19922-12fqiwz.pdf?AWSAccessKeyId=AKIAIWOWYYGZ2Y53UL3A&Expires=1537531436&Signature=5Whcd%2BZwbQetWjRAS2%2FGzjW2

rXo%3D&response-content-disposition=inline%3B%20-
filename%3DComorbid_physical_health_conditions_and.pdf.

Examined Existence. (2018). *10 Intriguing Facts about Anxiety*.
[online] Available at: https://examinedexistence.com/10-
intriguing-facts-about-anxiety/ [Accessed 30 Jul. 2018].

Eyre, H., 2017, Zayn Malik: *Love Hurts ... Love is Hard, The
Times*, [online]. Available at: www.thetimes.co.uk/article/
zayn-malik-on-gigi-hadid-bradford-pillowtalk-one-direction-
65kvx3d3v [accessed 23rd January 2019]

Field, G. (2015). *Sarah Silverman Opens Up About Her Battle
With Depression and Her Gutsiest Career Move Yet*. [online]
Glamour. Available at: www.glamour.com/story/sarah-
silverman-on-i-smile-back-and-battle-with-depression
[Accessed 23 Jan. 2019].

Files.digital.nhs.uk. (2018). [online] Available at: https://files.
digital.nhs.uk/pdf/t/6/adult_psychiatric_study_ch2_web.pdf
[Accessed 30 Jul. 2018].

**Fogliati, V., Terides, M., Gandy, M., Staples, L., Johnston,
L., Karin, E., Rapee, R., Titov, N. and Dear, B**. (2016).
Psychometric properties of the mini-social phobia inventory
(Mini-SPIN) in a large online treatment-seeking sample.
Cognitive Behaviour Therapy, [online] 45(3), pp.236–57.
Available at: www.tandfonline.com/doi/full/10.1080/1650607
3.2016.1158206 [Accessed 7 Aug. 2018].

Galloway, S. (2012). *THR Cover: Confessions of Ben Affleck*.
[online] The Hollywood Reporter. Available at:
www.hollywoodreporter.com/news/ben-affleck-thr-cover-
argo-oscar-377611 [Accessed 23 Jan. 2019].

Grewal, R. and George, T. (2017). *Cannabis-Induced
Psychosis: A Review | Psychiatric Times*. [online]
Psychiatrictimes.com. Available at: www.psychiatrictimes.
com/substance-use-disorder/cannabis-induced-psychosis-
review [Accessed 7 Aug. 2018].

Heysigmund.com. (2018). *An Unexpected Way to Deal with Performance Anxiety*. [online] Available at: www.heysigmund.com/an-unexpected-way-to-deal-with-performance-anxiety/ [Accessed 30 Jul. 2018].

Hqip.org.uk. (2017). *Suicide by Children and Young People*. [online] Available at: www.hqip.org.uk/wp-content/uploads/2018/02/report-suicide-by-children-and-young-people-in-england.pdf [Accessed 30 Jul. 2018].

Hunt, J. and Eisenberg, D. (2010). Mental Health Problems and Help-Seeking Behavior Among College Students. *Journal of Adolescent Health*, [online] 46(1), pp.3-10. Available at: www.jahonline.org/article/S1054-139X(09)00340-1/fulltext [Accessed 1 Aug. 2018].

Icd.who.int. (2018). *ICD-11 – Mortality and Morbidity Statistics*. [online] Available at: https://icd.who.int/browse11/l-m/en#/http%3a%2f%2fid.who.int%2ficd%2fentity%2f334423054 [Accessed 29 Jul. 2018].

IPPR (2017). *Not by Degrees*. [online] IPPR. Available at: www.ippr.org/files/2017-09/1504645674_not-by-degrees-170905.pdf [Accessed 9 Aug. 2018].

Kearns, M., Muldoon, O., Msetfi, R. and Surgenor, P. (2015). Understanding help-seeking amongst university students: the role of group identity, stigma, and exposure to suicide and help-seeking. *Frontiers in Psychology*, [online] 6. Available at: www.ncbi.nlm.nih.gov/pmc/articles/PMC4586350/ [Accessed 1 Aug. 2018].

Knott, L. (2018). *Acute Stress Reaction | Stress Advice*. [online] Patient.info. Available at: https://patient.info/health/stress-management/acute-stress-reaction [Accessed 29 Jul. 2018].

Krusemark, E., Novak, L., Gitelman, D. and Li, W. (2013). When the Sense of Smell Meets Emotion: Anxiety-State-Dependent Olfactory Processing and Neural Circuitry Adaptation. *Journal of Neuroscience*, 33(39), pp.15324–32

Lane, J., Adcock, R., Williams, R. and Kuhn, C. (1990). Caffeine effects on cardiovascular and neuroendocrine responses to acute psychosocial stress and their relationship to level of habitual caffeine consumption. *Psychosomatic Medicine*, [online] 52(3), pp.320–36. Available at: www.ncbi. nlm.nih.gov/pubmed/2195579 [Accessed 9 Aug. 2018].

Lipson, S., Jones, J., Taylor, C., Wilfley, D., Eichen, D., Fitzsimmons-Craft, E. and Eisenberg, D. (2017). Understanding and promoting treatment-seeking for eating disorders and body image concerns on college campuses through online screening, prevention and intervention. *Eating Behaviors*, [online] 25, pp.68–73. Available at: www.ncbi.nlm. nih.gov/pubmed/27117825 [Accessed 1 Aug. 2018].

Mackay, G. and Neill, J. (2010). The effect of "green exercise" on state anxiety and the role of exercise duration, intensity, and greenness: A quasi-experimental study. *Psychology of Sport and Exercise*, [online] 11(3), pp.238–45. Available at: www.sciencedirect.com/science/article/pii/ S1469029210000038?via%3Dihub [Accessed 9 Aug. 2018].

May, R. (1977). *The meaning of anxiety by Rollo May*. New York: Norton.

MedicinesComplete. (2018). *Access leading drug and healthcare references – MedicinesComplete*. [online] Available at: www.medicinescomplete.com/#/content/bnf/_819609181 [Accessed 7 Aug. 2018].

Mind.org.uk. (2018). *Anxiety symptoms | Mind, the mental health charity – help for mental health problems*. [online] Available at: www.mind.org.uk/information-support/types-of-mental-health-problems/anxiety-and-panic-attacks/anxiety-symptoms/#.W17zAy2ZMdU [Accessed 30 Jul. 2018].

My Body and Soul. (2017). *This is What Emma Stone Wants You to Know About Anxiety, My Body and Soul* [online]. Available at: www.bodyandsoul.com.au/mind-body/wellbeing/this-is-what-

emma-stone-wants-you-to-know-about-anxiety/news-sto
ry/9b72237712256481062031c79ede6e32 [accessed 23rd
January 2019]

**Niles, A., Haltom, K., Mulvenna, C., Lieberman, M.
and Stanton, A**. (2013). Randomized controlled trial of
expressive writing for psychological and physical health: the
moderating role of emotional expressivity. *Anxiety, Stress, &
Coping*, [online] 27(1), pp.1–17. Available at: www.ncbi.nlm.
nih.gov/pubmed/23742666 [Accessed 18 Sep. 2018].

Our World in Data. (2018). *Mental Health*. [online] Available
at: https://ourworldindata.org/mental-health [Accessed 30
Jul. 2018].

Pathways.nice.org.uk. (2018). *Common mental health
disorders in primary care – NICE Pathways*. [online] Available
at: https://pathways.nice.org.uk/pathways/common-mental-
health-disorders-in-primary-care [Accessed 7 Aug. 2018].

Publishing, H. (2018). *Understanding the stress response –
Harvard Health*. [online] Harvard Health. Available at:
www.health.harvard.edu/staying-healthy/understanding-
the-stress-response [Accessed 29 Jul. 2018].

Ray, A. (2010). *Om chanting and meditation*. Lexington, KY:
Inner Light Publishers.

Rcpsych.ac.uk. (2018). *Anxiety panic phobias*. [online]
Available at: www.rcpsych.ac.uk/expertadvice/problems/
anxietyphobias/anxiety,panic,phobias.aspx [Accessed 29 Jul.
2018].

Reinhart, L. (2017). *Lili Reinhart on Instagram: "YOU are
the one thing in this world, above all other things, that you
must never give up on. When I was in middle school, I was
struggling...".* [online] Instagram. Available at:
www.instagram.com/lilireinhart/p/BY4PnRjgBqI/ [Accessed
23 Jan. 2019].

Scott, K., Bruffaerts, R., Tsang, A., Ormel, J., Alonso, J., Angermeyer, M., Benjet, C., Bromet, E., de Girolamo, G., de Graaf, R., Gasquet, I., Gureje, O., Haro, J., He, Y., Kessler, R., Levinson, D., Mneimneh, Z., Oakley Browne, M., Posada-Villa, J., Stein, D., Takeshima, T. and Von Korff, M. (2007). Depression–anxiety relationships with chronic physical conditions: Results from the World Mental Health surveys. *Journal of Affective Disorders*, [online] 103(1-3), pp.113–20. Available at: https://s3.amazonaws. com/academia.edu.documents/45252427/Depression- anxiety_relationships_with_ch20160501-23987-1o5zef9.pd f?AWSAccessKeyId=AKIAIWOWYYGZ2Y53UL3A&Expires=1 537531721&Signature=9rOZs1kGIYHJh%2FVAtBSk%2B0a %2BsOs%3D&response-content-disposition=inline%3B%- 20filename%3DDepression_anxiety_relationships_with_ ch.pdf.

The Guardian (2018). *Doctors warn of rise in people seeking help over prescription pills bought online*. [online] Available at: www.theguardian.com/society/2018/jul/13/doctors-warn-of- rise-in-addiction-to-prescription-drugs-bought-online-xanax [Accessed 1 Aug. 2018].

Thorley, C. (2017). *Not by Degrees*. [online] IPPR. Available at: www.ippr.org/files/2017-09/1504645674_not-by- degrees-170905.pdf [Accessed 29 Jul. 2018].

Van Voorhees, B., Fogel, J., Houston, T., Cooper, L., Wang, N. and Ford, D. (2006). Attitudes and illness factors associated with low perceived need for depression treatment among young adults. *Social Psychiatry and Psychiatric Epidemiology*, [online] 41(9), pp.746–54. Available at: www.researchgate.net/publication/6889721_Attitudes_ and_illness_factors_associated_with_low_perceived_need_ for_depression_treatment_among_young_adults [Accessed 1 Aug. 2018].

**If you found this book interesting ...
why not read these next?**

Doing Single Well

**A Guide to Living, Loving and
Dating without compromise**

Doing Single Well will help you find fulfilment
in your single life, and if you want a partner,
to wait for one who is right for you.

Body Image Problems
& Body Dysmorphic Disorder

The Definitive Treatment and Recovery Approach

This unique and inspiring book provides simple yet highly
effective self-help methods to help you overcome your body
image concerns and Body Dysmorphic Disorder (BDD).

the _Shaw_ mind
FOUNDATION

Creating hope for children,
adults and families

Sign up to our charity, The Shaw Mind Foundation

www.shawmindfoundation.org

and keep in touch with us; we would love to hear
from you.

*Our goal is to make help and support available for every
single person in society, from all walks of life.
We will never stop offering hope. These are our promises.*

TRIGGER™
The mental health & wellbeing publisher

www.triggerpublishing.com

Trigger is a publishing house devoted to opening conversations about mental health. We tell the stories of people who have suffered from mental illnesses and recovered, so that others may learn from them.

Adam Shaw is a worldwide mental health advocate and philanthropist. Now in recovery from mental health issues, he is committed to helping others suffering from debilitating mental health issues through the global charity he co-founded, The Shaw Mind Foundation. www.shawmindfoundation.org

Lauren Callaghan (CPsychol, PGDipClinPsych, PgCert, MA (hons), LLB (hons), BA), born and educated in New Zealand, is an innovative industry-leading psychologist based in London, United Kingdom. Lauren has worked with children and young people, and their families, in a number of clinical settings providing evidence based treatments for a range of illnesses, including anxiety and obsessional problems. She was a psychologist at the specialist national treatment centres for severe obsessional problems in the UK and is renowned as an expert in the field of mental health, recognised for diagnosing and successfully treating OCD and anxiety related illnesses in particular. In addition to appearing as a treating clinician in the critically acclaimed and BAFTA award-winning documentary *Bedlam*, Lauren is a frequent guest speaker on mental health conditions in the media and at academic conferences. Lauren also acts as a guest lecturer and honorary researcher at the Institute of Psychiatry Kings College, UCL.

Please visit the link below:
www.triggerpublishing.com

Join us and follow us...

@triggerpub
@Shaw_Mind

Search for us on Facebook